How To Create Awesome Meetings

*A Step-By-Step Guide
to help you make your next meeting
more productive & profitable.*

GORD SHEPPARD

Create Awesome Meetings

EDMONTON, CANADA

Gord Sheppard/Create Awesome Meetings
8426 76 St.
Edmonton, Alberta – Canada – T6C 2J9
www.createawesomemeetings.com

Book Layout © 2014 BookDesignTemplates.com

To book Gord Sheppard for a meeting facilitation, speaking or consulting engagement, visit www.createawesomemeetings.com

How To Create Awesome Meetings/Gord Sheppard -- 1st ed.
ISBN 978-0-9949291-0-5

Changing the world, one meeting at a time.

Contents

1

Foreword

If you want your next meeting to be more productive and profitable then you're in the right place, because I have a knack for helping people create exceptional meetings.

> "Over the years, I have been part of numerous planning sessions, but I have to say that Gord's ability to get straight to the point and see through all of the cloudiness is inspirational. He has an uncanny gift of being able to read individuals and situations, while bringing out their best in a very short amount of time. He helped us to produce great results that are truly actionable."[1]
>
> *Cynthia Annett, Board Chair*
> *Special Olympics Edmonton*

I have written "How To Create Awesome Meetings" because I want to help you get the most from all of your meetings. This book is for executives who are at their wit's end when it comes to meetings. It's for managers who dread their weekly staff meetings. It's for non-profit volunteers who want board meetings that respect their precious time. This book is also for anyone who wants to yell out "STOP! This meeting is a waste of my time! I'm leaving!"

I have facilitated, run and participated in more than 2000 meetings. During that time I have experienced just about everything that could happen in a meeting. So now I want to pass along my best insights to help you make your next meeting awesome. So, if you're ready to say goodbye to wasted time, useless conflicts, lost profits, and listening to another co-worker talk about the latest cat video, then "How To Create Awesome Meetings" is the ultimate step-by-step guide that will help you make your next meeting more productive and profitable!

Sincerely,

Gord Sheppard

2

Why Create Awesome Meetings

Meetings Connect Us All

If you think about it, everything we do is connected by a meeting.

For example, some time after your parents first met they had an intimate meeting, which is how you got started. Then they met with a doctor or a mid-wife and you were born. After that, your lifelong meeting train left the station and never stopped. You had childhood meetings with doctors, teachers, principals, boy scout leaders, dance instructors, coaches, girlfriends, boyfriends and anyone else who had an influence on your life. Somewhere in your teens you probably met your first employer, which led to another series of meetings, including negotiation, orientation, termination and so on. Then, if you went to college, you met with friends, clubs, teams, professors, etc. Now you're working for a company, or for yourself, which of course includes all kinds of meetings with staff, clients, suppliers, and many other people. Oh, and you're probably a volunteer, which also involves meeting with...you get the picture.

So if we've all been in so many meetings then we should be pretty good at them by now. Right?

When A Meeting Goes Well...

- We feel great
- We accomplish our goals
- We want to meet again

When A Meeting Goes Poorly...

- We feel bad
- Nothing gets accomplished
- We don't want to meet again, and when we do meet again we don't give our best effort

What Would Happen If...

- You could have consistently productive meetings?
- You felt great about every meeting you went to?
- You could stop in the middle of your next meeting and link what you're doing in that moment to your organization strategy?

Why I Create Awesome Meetings

I love my work as a Professional Meeting Facilitator and Consultant. Why? Because helping people conduct effective meetings enables them to perform at their best and strengthen their business at the same time. It also energizes people and puts big smiles on their faces. So to help you make your next meeting more productive and profitable I wrote this book to pass along everything that I have learned. I also hope it puts a smile on your face.

When I facilitate an effective meeting I work with senior leaders before, during and after the event. We begin by clarifying the organization strategy and linking it to what will happen in the meeting. We also talk about how to help each individual perform at his or her best when we meet. During the meeting I keep everyone focused on key issues and don't allow any personality barriers to get in the way. I also ensure that each person states what he or she is going to do after leaving the room. Afterwards, I work with the senior leaders to consolidate what we learned and link it to their strategic objectives. This process ensures that the meeting made their business more profitable.

And honestly, I haven't always loved meetings. In fact I would say that of the 2000+ meetings that I have run and participated in throughout my lifetime, I only really began to enjoy them when I became a Professional Meeting Facilitator. One of the main reasons that I am driven to help you make your next meeting awesome is because of the countless, poorly run corporate meetings that I had to endure throughout my career. Those meetings had all the typical bad meeting problems, including poor facilitation, no agenda, infighting, open sexism and raised voices, among other issues. But worst of all was how I behaved during so many of those poorly run meetings. Because I was often either tuned out or resistant. So now, when I facilitate an event, I am on the lookout for 'old me'. When I meet 'old me' in a meeting I can steer him away from being resistant to becoming an enthusiastic participant who wants to make the meeting better.

So I hope that you use this book to:

- Avoid the 'old me'
- Take advantage of the many insights that I have gained by surviving thousands of meetings
- Make your next meeting awesome!

And if that's not enough, here are a few more reasons why you should create awesome meetings.

Get Our $ Billions Back!

It's hard to fathom how much money we're all losing because of bad meetings. According to www.BusinessInsider.com[2] unproductive meetings cost more than $37 billion per year in the United States alone! Think about that on a global scale. Bad meetings could be burning more than $1 trillion a year around the world! If we could make bad meetings the new 'smoking' and we all worked to reduce our addiction, can you imagine how much money we could save?

Get Your $ Thousands Back!

What type of meeting are you in most often? How much does it cost? Here are a few estimates to help you think about the value of your next meeting:

- Weekly staff meeting - 1 hour = $1,000+
- Non-profit board meeting - 1 hour = $2,000+
- Executive monthly meeting - 1 hour = $5,000+
- Corporate board meeting - 1 hour = $10,000+

Note: These estimates don't even include preparation time!

Now take a look around your next meeting and add up the total cost per hour like this:

$ Wages per hour + $ Meeting Space Cost + $ Refreshments = $ Total Meeting Cost per hour

Example:

+ $ Wages for 8 people = $1,500 per hour
+ $ Room Rental, Heat, Audio/Visual Equipment = $300 per hour
+ $ Muffins/Bagels/Coffee = $50
= $ A Total Meeting Cost of $1,850 for one hour!

Keep that total meeting cost in mind the next time somebody talks for 20 minutes about his or her favourite cat video!

Get Your Time Back!

"That meeting was a complete waste of time!"

Sound familiar? Then do something about it!

Get Your Sanity Back!

Bad meetings will drive you crazy! Sometimes people fight, or worse, they don't care. Sometimes people are too chatty, too quiet, too loud, and all you want to do is scream out loud to make the useless meeting stop! How much longer are you willing to lose your mind in bad meetings?

Meetings Are Your Early Warning System

Like sending a canary into a coalmine to check for deadly gases, meetings can be an early warning system for how your business is performing. At their best, meetings will produce your most innovative and successful products and services. At their worst, meetings can be counter-productive snake pits that waste a lot of time and money. At their absolute worst, meetings can be OK. You know the kind of meeting that I'm talking about? The one where people are just going through the motions and things sort of get done? So if you want to know how your company is performing, just ask your people how their meetings are going. Then ask...

- If our meetings are already effective, how can we make them even better?
- Can we afford any more bad meetings?
- What would happen if we created awesome meetings?

The Answer Is In Your Hands!

'How To Create Awesome Meetings' is a step-by-step guide that provides the tools, information and inspiration to help you execute the most profitable and productive meetings in your industry.

This Step-By-Step Guide Will Help You

- Turn your meetings into a competitive advantage
- Inspire you to improve your communication abilities
- Help everyone on your team fall in love with meetings and more!

Who This Book Is For

- Corporate Executives
- Managers
- Government Leaders
- Board Directors
- Non-Profit Leaders

- Small Business Owners
- Employees
- Volunteers
- 'Old Me,' as in, the guy who's being a jerk in meetings because he thinks he knows it all and believes that bad meetings are everybody else's fault

How To Use This Step-By-Step Guide

This book is based on the "10 Ways To Create Awesome Meetings Checklist ✓" As you work your way through this book you can use the checklist to mark your progress as you complete each step. There are two ways to get a copy of this list.

1. You can use the short version listed here:

"10 Ways To Create Awesome Meetings Checklist ✓"

1. Get Real With Yourself
2. Get Real With Your Team
3. Know Your Total Meeting Cost $
4. Get A Great Facilitator
5. Link The Meeting To Your Strategy
6. Build A Blockbuster A-G-E-N-D-A
7. Meet In The Right Space
8. Get Awesome Meeting Resources
9. Follow-up F-A-S-T
10. Take Action!

2. You can get the long version that includes a set of bonus questions to help you be even more prepared as you go into your next meeting. To get the long version go to www.createawesomemeetings.com and enter your name and email into the subscriber list. Then a copy of the "10 Ways To Create Awesome Meetings Checklist ✓" will be sent to you.

You can also work through this guide all at once or use each step as needed. It's up to you.

Are Bad Meetings Keeping You Awake At Night?

If bad meetings are hurting you and your organization, then you need to do something about it! You can get started by putting this step-by-step guide into action. Then, when your meetings become more productive and profitable, you can look forward to getting a better sleep.

Getting Started Is Easier Than You Think

While you may not be able to fix your meeting problems all at once, "How To Create Awesome Meetings" will enable you and your team to achieve the small wins that you need to build more productive and profitable meetings.

And if you need help please get in touch with me at gord@createawesomemeetings.com. You can also take advantage of all the great meeting resources on www.createawesomemeetings.com

3

Step 1: Get Real With Yourself

Great Meetings Start With You

Before you go to your next meeting, take a look in the mirror and ask yourself...

- How do I act during a meeting?
- How do I *want* to act during a meeting?

If you like what you hear then please move on to the next chapter. If you don't like what you're saying to yourself then read on. Because the whole point of the first step is to help you gain the self-awareness you need to be your best in every meeting you attend.

My Meeting Story

I have facilitated, run and participated in more than 2000 meetings. Looking back, I can honestly say that it wasn't until meeting number 1500 that I truly began to take responsibility for how I acted. Around that time I was a corporate employee and I thought I knew it all. If a meeting went well, then I took the credit. If the meeting went badly, then I blamed my manager, or the client, or my co-workers. Basically, I believed that it was everyone else's fault but mine.

When I look back at my behaviour, especially during some of those weekly staff meetings, I feel embarrassed. Because if I didn't like how a discussion was going I would cross my arms, lean back in my chair and be huffy. If I didn't like what someone said then I would openly disagree with that person. One of the worst things that I did to sabotage some of my managers was to avoid answering his or her questions. If I did give an answer, it was intentionally vague and not helpful. Part of why I acted this way was because I often didn't like the managers. But that is no excuse. The truth is that I wasn't taking responsibility for myself during those meetings.

I wish I had read Victor Frankl's book, "Man's Search For Meaning"[3] a lot sooner in my life. In 1944, Victor Frankl was taken prisoner by the Nazis and put into a concentration camp. During that time, he made a remarkable discovery. He learned that he could choose how he felt about what was happening to him regardless of how he was being treated. So even though he was being tortured and starved, and people around him were being murdered, he understood that he could choose his attitude toward the situation.

"Between stimulus and response there is a space. In that space is our power to choose our response. In our response lies our growth and our freedom."

Viktor Frankl
Neurologist and Psychiatrist[4]

While I wish I'd gained this wisdom sooner, I am so grateful that I understand the concept now and that I can apply it to myself, my clients and my family.

Speaking of family, you know who helped me to begin to take responsibility for myself? My wife. Because one fateful day when I was complaining endlessly about those meetings she told me to "Just Stop It!" It was too much for her to handle. I was driving her crazy because I was complaining about the same things over and over again and not doing anything about it (isn't that the definition of insanity?).

Wow. What a waste of time.

So if there is one message that you take away from this whole book I hope it is this:

You can choose how you act during a meeting

Your Meeting Story?

Good. Bad. Ugly. No matter what's happening in your meetings imagine how you would feel if you could choose your reaction? For example, if you're having the most inno-vative company meetings ever, then you could choose to go into those meetings with even greater enthusiasm to keep the momentum going. Or, if you're part of a bad weekly meeting, then you could begin to shift how you feel about it by asking yourself...

- How do I act during a meeting?
- How do I *want* to act during a meeting?

Once you have answered these questions then you can go deeper and ask yourself...

- How do I feel about other people in the meeting?
- How do others feel about me?

- What do I want from this meeting?
- What is my role in the meeting?
- How can I influence the meeting?

It doesn't matter if you're the leader, follower, facilitator or the note taker. How you act during a meeting is up to you.

Taking control of how you act starts by getting real with yourself.

So what do you want to do about it?

Get Real Faster

It took me way too long to take responsibility for myself in meetings. So please don't wait!

Not only did becoming self-aware help me to grow per-sonally, it also helped me to become an excellent meeting facilitator. So I hope you're able to understand and guide your own behaviour so that you can influence your next meeting in a positive way. Because how much longer can you afford not to try your best? What would happen if you approached all of you gatherings with passion and integrity? How would you benefit? How would your team benefit? How would your company's profits benefit?

Getting real with yourself is a process. Understanding yourself requires time, self-reflection and great resources. To find the information you need you can start by asking friends, family and colleagues for help. You may also want to consult with a medical professional. In my own experi-ence I have also used the following self-discovery tools with great success, and I hope that you find them useful as you discover how to get real with yourself.

Real Personality Assessments

Personality assessments can help you understand your-self at a deeper level. Among the many personality assessments you can look into, two of the most reputable are:

- Myers Briggs Type Indicator (MBTI)[5]
- True Colors[6]

According to Myers Briggs (which I have taken twice) my personality type is ENTP. This basically means that I'm an upbeat visionary who obsesses too much over minor details and loves to talk a lot. Learning this about myself has helped me perform better in meetings because:

- I now know that I am skilled at seeing the big picture and can do a good job of tying discussions together
- I know I work well with people who enjoy detail and I have to be mindful of other visionary types in a meet-ing
- I now understand that if I talk less during a meeting then quiet people will have a better chance to share their valuable ideas

Hopefully, you can use the results of a personality test to change how you act during a meeting for the better. And no matter which personality assessment you choose, you should have it administered by a certified professional. You will also want to keep a copy of your personality test results nearby to remind yourself about how to optimize your

behaviour so you can be more productive at your next
meeting.

**A Fun Way To Use Your Personality Assessment Re-
sults**

If you did the Myers Briggs Type Indicator Personality
Test and you now know your personality type, then I suggest you have some fun by checking out websites like
www.CelebrityTypes.com[7]. This website lists celebrities who
have the same personality type as you. For example, when
I looked up 'ENTP's I found out that Robert Downey Jr. and
Jon Stewart are ENTPs just like me. Knowing that I have the
same traits as these Hollywood stars makes for a great conversation starter whenever I'm meeting new people.

Get Real Mentors

Want to really get to know yourself? Get a mentor. Because a strong mentor will tell you when you're right or
wrong or getting in your own way. He or she will also
quickly understand your key issues and offer honest feedback you can use before and after you make important
decisions. For example, if you're frustrated that you didn't
get to state your opinion during a meeting, then you could
bring this up with your mentor. Your mentor might suggest
other ways to help you be heard, or he or she might recommend that you let this point go and move on.

Learn How To Ask

Asking for help is hard for many people. So you should
practice how to ask before reaching out to a potential
mentor. You can also expect to be turned down a few times

before you find the right person. But if you realize that there are many people in your immediate circle of contacts who want to help you, especially if their time will be well used because they are going to see you get positive results, then you shouldn't hesitate to reach out.

Mentorship Is A Two-Way Street

Great mentorship is a two-way street. So when you ask someone to become your mentor you have to be clear with each other about why you're getting into this relationship. The mentor will likely want to 'give back' and 'see you succeed,' because being a mentor is often a selfish act where the mentor gets as much out of giving guidance as you do from receiving it. You also have to be honest about what you really want from your mentor. Otherwise, both of you will become frustrated.

How To Work With Your Mentor

Set up three meetings. Then you and your mentor can agree on an agenda for the first meeting. When you meet, you should carry out the agenda and stay focused. If you want to socialize after the meeting, that's fine, but for the hour that you spend together you will want to concentrate on the issues that need to be solved. Then, after three meetings, you can reflect back on how productive the relationship has been and decide on whether or not to continue.

Mentors Are Invaluable

What if your mentor was like my wife and didn't put up with any of your useless complaining? What if he or she gave you straight advice that helped you improve how you act during meetings, which then made every meeting that you attend better? Many successful business people acknowledge that the advice that they receive from mentors helps them to grow and to positively influence their organizations.

> "I've seen that phenomenally successful people believe they can learn something from everybody. I call them 'mavericks with mentors.' Richard Branson, for instance, is a total maverick but he surrounds himself with incredibly successful, smart people and he listens to them."[8]
>
> *Brendon Burchard, Author*

How long can you afford not to have a mentor?

Who Will Your Next Mentor Be?

You can start your search for a mentor by asking friends and family for suggestions. You could also target specific people at work and offer to buy them a coffee so you can chat. This will allow you to find out if they would be interested or if they know anyone else who might want to be your mentor. There are also many organizations that you can research to find mentors, including:

- **Million Women Mentors**[9] that "Supports the engagement of one million science, technology, engineering and math (STEM) mentors (male and female) to increase the interest and confidence of girls and women to persist and succeed in STEM programs and careers."

- **The Esquire Mentoring Initiative**[10] asks "Who Made You The Man You Are Today?" and it offers great resources and inspiration from famous men to help you learn more about mentoring
- And don't hesitate to contact your local **Business Association, Municipal/State/Provincial Government** or **Volunteer Association** for guidance

Wayne Gretzky[11], the most successful hockey player of all time, had his Dad, Walter Gretzky[12]. Oprah Winfrey[13] had her fourth grade teach Mrs. Duncan[14]. Who will your next mentor be? What impact will he or she have on how you act during your next meeting?

"If I have seen further it is by standing on the shoulders of giants."[15]

Isaac Newton
Physicist and Mathematician

Step 1: Conclusion

If there is one thing that I hope you remember about getting real with yourself when it comes to meetings, it's this:

You can choose how you act during a meeting

I also hope that you learn this as quickly as possible so that you and your whole meeting team can benefit. As a reminder, jot down the top three self-awareness tips that you need to know before your next meeting:

1.

2.

3.

Then, after your meeting, you can follow up and track your progress for each self-awareness tip here:

1.

2.

3.

And whatever you choose to do about this, just do it! Take a personality test. Conduct research. Find a mentor. Talk to your family and friends or a medical professional. Basically, do whatever you can to get out of your own way and become the type of person you were meant to be during meetings. Because, ultimately, you are responsible for these two questions...

- How do I act during a meeting?
- How do I *want* to act during a meeting?

Tip: Check out 'Worksheet #1' in the Appendix of this guide to get a blank copy of the 'Top 3 Self Awareness Reminders'

Step 1: Get Real With Yourself Checklist √

1. Do I understand how I act during a meeting?
2. Do I know how I *want* to act during a meeting?
3. Have I talked with my friends, family, colleagues and a medical professional about how to become more self-aware?
4. What are the top three things that I have to

remember about myself that will help me make my next meeting better?

5. How could a personality assessment help me?
6. Do I want a mentor?
7. Do I understand how to find a mentor and how to make a mentoring relationship successful?
8. Will I actually set aside the proper amount of time it will take to really get to know myself better?
9. How will I celebrate progress as I gain self-awareness?
10. How will I demonstrate that the new way that I act during meetings is making my organization stronger?

Tip: Check out Step 8 in this guide to find more awesome resources that will help you 'Get Real With Yourself'

Up Next

Now that you've gotten real with yourself, you're ready to take on "Step 2: Get Real With Your Team."

4

Step 2: Get Real With Your Team

Get Real Faster

Because I have facilitated, run and participated in more than 2000 meetings, I know firsthand what happens when people don't fix problems quickly:

- Projects slow down
- People hold back important information
- People avoid meetings or don't fully participate when they attend
- There can be serious personal fights
- Enough bad meetings in a row can cause some of your best people to dust off their resumes and start looking for work elsewhere
- Profits are lost

Sound familiar?

Ironically, most people know what's wrong with their meetings and they even know how to fix the problems. But they can't take action because they can't get real with each other. For example, in my own career I have experienced bad team meeting behaviours that:

- Destroyed a new business because the partners

fought too much during meetings
- Held back a non-profit from raising millions because everyone on the board was too nice during meetings so they never got anything done
- Turned an entire corporate department of workers into 'Yes Men' who didn't say anything important during the dreaded 'weekly staff meeting' because it was the only way to survive

On the flip-side I have also experienced exceptional team meeting behaviours that:

- Helped a business owner to be more open and honest with his staff, which in turn created a collaborative environment that led to new ideas that helped the owner get out of debt and grow his business
- Fostered an innovative discussion from which a new restaurant was born

If great team meetings can help you achieve your most important goals, including higher profits, happier staff, more productive volunteers and other benefits, then what are you waiting for?

Get A Real Team Meeting Ranking

Rank the performance of your team on a scale of 1-10 based on the team meeting behaviours listed here.

1-4/10 - A Low Score

Team Meeting Behaviours Include:

- Low trust

- Open conflict
- No agenda
- People are late
- Too much talking about personal issues
- Checking phones during meeting
- Offensive comments
- Jokes/language in poor taste
- Output of the meeting is poor

5-8/10 - An Average Score

Team Meeting Behaviours Include:

- Basic level of trust
- Consistent and orderly
- Follow the agenda well
- Everybody is nice
- There may be some conflicts but nobody talks about it
- Output of the meeting produces average results

9-10/10 - Outstanding Score

Team Meeting Behaviours Include:

- High level of trust
- Healthy conflicts
- Confident leader/facilitator
- Everybody contributes and tries their best
- Innovative ideas happen often
- People encourage each other
- People laugh out loud
- People can't wait for the next meeting
- The meetings improve profitability

Write your current team score here:

_____ / 10

Write what you want your team score to become here:

_____ / 10

Some People Gotta Grow And Some People Gotta Go

Before you can achieve what you want your new team score to be, you have to deal with who is actually on the team. Because we all understand that having the right people in a meeting is one of the best ways to succeed. But why do so many leaders struggle with this issue?

Desperation - Sometimes the economy is hot and it's hard to get good people, so managers hire staff that aren't a good fit. In the non-profit sector, organizations are often so desperate to get volunteers that they recruit volunteer board members who don't have the competencies to help the organization achieve its goals.

Switching Costs - You might think that firing your current employee and hiring a new person will cost too much money and take took much time. As a result, you put up with your current employee's bad behaviour during meetings.

High Pain Tolerance - Many leaders put up with a high level of mediocrity, even when they know they should get rid of a bad apple on their team. This is usually because the leader is uncomfortable with confrontation.

So before you get real with your meeting team you have to decide who's 'gotta grow' and 'who's gotta go.'

Some People Gotta Grow – Some of your people only need a little bit of guidance to become awesome contributors to your meetings. Don't wait to do something about this! Creating and executing a growth plan for each staff member, or volunteer, will deepen his or her commitment to your organization and help you recruit new people more easily because they'll hear about how much your current employees are learning, growing and contributing.

Some People Gotta Go – We all understand this. So stop being so nice and find a lawful and respectful way to dismiss your poor-performing employees. Because if you don't get rid of the dead wood, then your high performers may become frustrated and quit, and your meetings will get even worse.

Take Action!

If learning how to be authentic is the only thing holding your team back from having more productive and profitable meetings, then take action! To help you do this I have put together the following steps to help you 'get real with your team.'
2A. How To Build Trust With Each Other
2B. How To Really Understand Each Person On The Team
2C. How To Become Awesome Listeners
2D. How To Make Sure Everybody Is Heard
2E. How To Support People For Who They Are
2F. Learn How To Fight
2G. How To Celebrate Getting Real With Your Team
2H. Invest Real Dollars To Grow Your Team

"If people like you, they'll listen to you. If they trust you, they'll do business with you."[16]

Zig Ziglar, Author, Salesman

Step 2A. How To Build Real Trust With Each Other

Building real team trust during a meeting starts with each person truly knowing themselves. One of the best ways to do this is to work through Step 1 in this guide. Then, once each individual has a solid level of self-understanding, you can begin to build overall team trust.

Ground Rules And Accountability

One of the easiest ways to build trust quickly is to establish meeting 'ground rules' for which each individual is accountable. These may include:

- Being on time
- Being prepared
- Turning off your phone
- Limiting personal story telling

No matter what ground rules you choose, making people accountable to each other for their actions is the only way to make them stick.

Do you remember when your parents didn't follow through and discipline you for behaving badly? Or how about when your teacher threatened the class and never did anything about it? I have seen too many helpless leaders curse a blue streak outside of a meeting instead of laying out real consequences and acting upon them. The result?

Projects slow down. Profits are lost. People only take care of themselves and the team gets left behind. Worst of all, you end up having a lot of useless meetings.

Go Deeper

If your team already has a basic level of confidence with each other, then here are a few suggestions for how you can deepen your trust even more:

- Ask each team member directly for his or her suggestions about how to improve trust during the meeting, and then follow up, take action, and be transparent about how these suggestions are being used
- Invest in an off-site team event. For example, you could book a conference room in a local hotel that also serves an excellent lunch. Then, because you are away from the office you are less likely to get interrupted, which will give you a great opportunity to get to know each other better
- Acknowledge the small wins that help you build team trust during each meeting. For example, if a quiet person speaks up for the first time, make sure that the group takes a moment to acknowledge that person's courage for doing something out of his or her comfort zone

Coach Carter

One of my favourite 'accountability' movies is *Coach Carter*, based on the real life story of basketball coach, Ken Carter[17]. In the film, a high school basketball coach helps his players get to college because he asks them to change their behaviour in a positive way. He does this by getting the entire team to sign a contract that lays out how they will behave, and then he makes them stick to it. The contract states that these young basketball players should maintain good grades, wear a tie on game day, and sit in the front row during every class, among other things.[18] When the kids break this contract, Coach Carter carries out the consequences by cancelling regular season basketball games in spite of community pressure not to do so. Eventually, everyone realizes that Coach Carter is being fair and acting in the best interests of the community, and the kids come together as a team.

Imagine how much more productive and profitable your meetings could be if your team actually stuck to its own 'ground rules.'

Real Team Trust Needs Real Consequences

So what will happen if someone in your next team meeting breaks a 'ground rule?'

- Will you fire them?
- Will they be asked to immediately leave the meeting?
- Will you say nothing during the meeting and then address it one-on-one after the meeting?
- Will you take away their phone?
- Will you make them publicly apologize?

If you don't do anything, how will that affect the rest of your team?

"Trust takes years to build, seconds to break and forever to repair."[19]

Author Unknown

Step 2B. How To Really Understand Each Person On The Team

Before you can build real team trust, you have to understand each person on the team.

Know Who Is In The Room

When I facilitate meetings I see the same types of personalities over and over again. Many of them are helpful, and some of them aren't. As you get to know who is in the room at your next meeting, see if you recognize anyone from this list:

- The Big Picture Person
- The Talker
- The Quiet One
- The Cheerleader
- The He-Who-Shares-Too-Much
- The Straight-To-The-Point-Person
- The Note Taker
- The Leader
- The Wanna-Be Leader
- Sneezy, Grumpy, Happy and anyone else who likes to sing 'Heigh- ho, heigh-ho, it's off to work we go...'

Balancing Out The Personalities

As a Professional Meeting Facilitator, I can quickly assess who is in the room and then work to get the best out of each personality type. For example, I can ask the 'Talker' to limit his or her comments and I can encourage the 'Quiet One' to share his or her insights. Balancing out the personalities in the room puts more focus on the issues. This takes the pressure off of people and allows for more robust discussions, which then leads to better business outcomes.

Questions To Ask To Get To Really Know Your Team

- Do we want to know more about each other?
- How well do you we need to know each other to make our next meeting awesome?
- What will happen if we don't get to know each other better?
- What activities can we do to get to know each other better?

Really Observe Each Other During Your Meeting

Getting to know each other during your meeting will help deepen mutual trust, which will lead to more innovative and profitable conversations. Here are some basic questions to ask about how each person acts during your meeting. Are they...

- Quiet or loud?
- Happy or sad?
- Social or do they keep to themselves?
- Leaders or followers?
- Idea generators?
- Idea enablers?
- Snappy dressers or slobs?
- Polite or crass?
- Listeners or talkers?
- On-time or late?
- Prepared or unprepared?
- Stinky or sweet smelling?

Get To Know Each Other Outside Of Your Meeting

Getting to know each other outside of your meeting can also help you to deepen team trust. Here are a few questions that your team members can ask each other in order to get this process started:

- Where are you from?
- What are your values?
- Do you do what you say you're going to do?
- Are you proactive or do you like to do things closer to a deadline?
- Are you a people person or do you like to work alone?
- Do you like potato chips or chocolate? Or both?

Exercise: You Be Me And I'll Be You

Temporarily switching identities can be a great way to really get to know each other. For example, you could have Susan from Accounting act like Eric from Human Resources for five minutes during a meeting. This would give Susan a chance to have some fun and exaggerate all of Eric's quirks. Often, this leads to laughter, but it can also get too personal, so make sure you have a strong facilitator who knows when to end the exercise. The facilitator should also point out why you did it, summarize what you learned about Eric, and link it back to your overall company strategy. For example, "Today, we learned that not only does Eric like to use complicated words, but we also discovered that everybody goes to him for advice. We're lucky to have Eric for this reason, and I can tell you that Eric demonstrates how to carry out our number one strategic objective of putting people first in this company."

And just so you know, I have also done this exercise with my family at home during dinner and we all laughed a lot!

Build A Meeting Team Traits Inventory (MTTI)

Building a Meeting Team Traits Inventory (MTTI) is a great way to identify the overall skill set of your team. The way to do this is to list the attributes of each person on your team. This snapshot will then allow you to see what skills you have available, and help you figure out which skills you need to be able to solve specific problems at your next meeting. Here's an example:

Meeting Team Traits Inventory Example

Meeting Description:

Innovation discovery meeting with the Corporate Executive Team

Meeting Goal:

Identify new products and services that will lead to new revenue streams

Available Team Traits For This Meeting:

- A few strong leaders
- Some overly quiet people
- Some negative people
- Some people who are too literal

Team Traits That We Need To Get For This Meeting:

- Idea challengers
- Innovative thinkers
- People who aren't afraid to speak their minds
- People who will follow up and take action

Observations:

- Because of the current combined attributes of this executive team, it will be difficult to have a productive innovation discussion
- Currently, there are no innovative thinkers and some of the key executives are reluctant to speak up during meetings

Action Items:

- Bring in an industry expert who has innovation experience
- Coach the quiet executives to help them learn how to speak up and share their best recommendations during the meeting

You can prepare a Meeting Team Traits Inventory for most gatherings, including weekly staff meetings, board meetings, and executive meetings.

Tip: Check out 'Worksheet #2' in the Appendix of this guide to get a blank copy of the 'Meeting Team Traits Inventory'

Proceed With Caution

When there is a high level of trust, doing a Meeting Team Traits Inventory can be very productive. On the other hand, if people misuse what they have learned about each other then it can be very damaging. For example, if someone who is dominant learned that someone else was mild-mannered, then the dominant person might take advantage of the situation. So I recommend that the Meeting Team Traits Inventory be developed by at least two people. This could include two people from the team or one person from the team and a human resource professional. Whatever combination you choose you will ensure that at least two perspectives are being considered, which is critical when you're dealing with sensitive information about your team members.

Set Your Meeting Team Up For Success

- You would never expect a college football team to win the Super Bowl
- You wouldn't ask your 8-year old to drive your car
- You wouldn't ask the cleaning staff to decide who should get laid off

So don't expect your meeting team to accomplish something that they don't have the ability to achieve. For example, if your current non-profit board volunteers don't have the marketing ability or contacts to raise millions of dollars, then you should hire a professional fundraiser. If your executive team doesn't know how to build a strategic plan then bring in a Management Consultant. Making sure that your team has the right combined skill set will allow you to tackle your toughest meeting challenges.

Make Real Time

"I don't have time to do a Meeting Team Traits

Inventory"

Really?

Many leaders think this type of approach is too time-consuming. Often, these are the same leaders who are frustrated about the poor results that their teams are producing during meetings.

How many more bad meetings can your organization afford?

Step 2C. How To Become Awesome Listeners

Get Interested

One of the biggest lessons that I learned at the Neighbourhood Playhouse Acting School in New York is that 'the most interesting people are those who are the most interested.' So how can you be the most interested person during your next team meeting, regardless of what people are talking about? Here are a few suggestions:

- If you're bored by what someone is saying then sharpen your focus by remembering the key things that you appreciate about them
- Take notes during the meeting and then afterwards you can connect with individuals and ask them to clarify what they were saying
- Work with your meeting leader to make sure that there isn't too much boring content in the meeting

Repeat What You've Heard

Another listening technique I learned in acting school was the art of repetition. For example, if someone says something during a meeting, one of the best ways to demonstrate that you heard that person is to repeat back what he or she said. And if you really want to deepen the connection then say that person's name when you repeat back what you've heard. Because hearing somebody else enthusiastically say your name can be the sweetest sound in the world.

Repetition Example

Imagine a company meeting in which James, the Vice President of Human Resources is talking with Bob, the Chief Financial Officer, during a monthly executive meeting.

JAMES: I recommend that we spend $250,000 to train 100 managers about change management in order to en-sure a smooth transition from the old manual time sheet entry system to the new Enterprise Resource Planning soft-ware system.
BOB: So James, you believe that spending $250,000 to train 100 managers will help us make a smooth transition to the new ERP Software System?
JAMES: Exactly.

Talk Less

Another way to become a great listener is to know when to shut up. Like the Greek Philosopher Epictetus said, "We have two ears and one mouth so that we can listen twice as much as we speak."[20] This is a great listening-to-speaking ratio to keep in mind for your next meeting. And if you think about it, you're already doing this with your best customers, so why not treat your meeting teammates with the same level of respect by listening more and talking less.

Real Listening Techniques

Here's a quick recap of the three ways to improve your listening skills:

1. Get interested
2. Repeat what you've heard and also say the person's name
3. Talk less

And here are a few more unique listening techniques you can use:

*   Make eye contact
*   Don't even think about checking your phone
*   Allow people to finish talking
*   Don't blurt out the solution before the speaker has stopped talking. Allow time to think about what that person has said before you answer. Or wait to respond after the meeting is over
*   Relax. Because if you're relaxed, then the speaker will feel more comfortable when making his or her point

Step 2D. How To Make Sure Everybody Is Heard

"The good and the wise lead quiet lives."[21]

Euripides, Athenian Playwright

One of the best ways to get real with your team is to ensure that everyone is heard during a meeting. Here are a few suggestions to help you do this.

Leverage The Agenda

One way to ensure that each person gets a chance to speak is to place each person's name on the agenda with a specific amount of time allotted to his or her turn. If the team member knows in advance when he or she will be asked to speak and for how long, then that person will be well prepared. The meeting leader could also do a brief introduction about what the person is about to say. This approach is especially effective with people who are reluctant to speak because the meeting leader is being openly supportive.

Leverage Communication Styles

Understand how each person prefers to communicate and then adjust for that during your meeting. For instance, you know that a 'Talker' won't have a problem speaking in public. You may also want to coach this type of person before the meeting to help him or her learn how to speak succinctly. Someone who is 'Quiet' may be terrified to speak during a meeting. A few ways to help this type of person include; allowing him or her to distribute a written version of his or her key points that could be read out by the facilitator during the meeting; allowing that person to prepare a slide presentation that carries most of his or her information and reduces the amount of time that person has to talk. You will also want to coach this type of person before the meeting to ensure that he or she feels confident enough to bring up his or her best ideas.

Leverage The Meeting Leader

Your meeting leader can ensure that everyone is heard by:

- Praising people when they make a great point during the meeting
- Allotting the appropriate amount of time for each person to speak, but still being flexible enough to allow someone who is making a great point to finish
- Respectfully interrupting anybody who tries to talk for too long or goes off topic
- Not playing favourites
- Modeling how to be heard, which may include making meaningful points in a short amount of time, keeping everyone on topic and being the most respectful person in the room

More Ways To Be Heard During A Meeting

In addition to leveraging the agenda and individual communication styles as well as your meeting leader, here are some additional suggestions that will help you to be heard during a meeting:

- Look for non-verbal cues. For example, if somebody is slouching tell that person to sit up straight to demonstrate that he or she is engaged
- Stop inappropriate language because it will cause many people to stop listening. And for your reference, one of the best remedies for bad language that I observed happened when I worked on a live TV show for kids. The TV hosts were not allowed to swear, especially if the camera was rolling. As a reminder to

not curse they had a 'swear jar' in the office and any time anybody swore they had to put a dollar in the jar. Pretty soon there was no more swearing in that office.

- Don't let anybody in a meeting speak too technically to be understood, because then people will stop listening and the technical person won't be heard
- Smell good. For my sake and everybody else's. Because I once worked for a manager who stunk, so it was very difficult to listen to him because all I could think about when he talked was the putrid stench caused by his body odor. How can you expect to be heard if you stink?

Make Your POINT

One of the best ways to make sure that you're heard during a meeting is to properly structure every POINT that you make. The following acronym explains what I mean.

- P - Prepare Your Idea
- O - Optimize The Benefits Of Your Idea
- I - Invite Feedback
- N - Name The Hurdles And Solutions
- T - Take Action

P-O-I-N-T Example

Imagine that the Chief Information Officer of a large company wants to present a better company-wide data analysis solution at a meeting. Here's how that person could make his or her P-O-I-N-T:

- **P - Prepare Your Idea** - At first that person will have to prepare, so he or she might do research, get opinions from colleagues, and then put all of the new information and insights together into a concise document

- **O - Optimize The Benefits Of Your Idea** - When that person pitches the idea during the next meeting then that person will have to bring his or her best ideas forward quickly. For example, that person might say, "Faster data will allow our company to make quicker decisions so it can leap ahead of our competition." To optimize this idea, that person will also have to invest it with passion and precision

- **I - Invite Feedback** - Now that person will have to stop talking and listen deeply so he or she can gather the positive and negative feedback about this idea. That person should also be taking notes and summarizing the main points made by his or her colleagues

- **N - Name The Hurdles And Solutions** - In this case the cost of implementation might be a hurdle, as well as the fact that the employees may not want to learn a new system. Solutions may include getting competitive bids for a new system, and surveying the employees to find out if they would actually oppose a new data analysis system. Naming hurdles and solutions is a critical part of making a solid POINT

- **T - Take Action** - Before anybody leaves the meeting, each person should state what he or she is going to do to move this issue forward. Then, at the next meeting, each person should report on the progress that he or she made.

Step 2E. How To Support People For Who They Are

As a young father I tried to shape my kids into what I thought they should become. When they didn't act the way I wanted, I would often raise my voice to try and get my way. It didn't work. I learned the hard way that you shouldn't do this with anybody, let alone your own kids. Thankfully, by the time they were midway through elementary school I figured out how to support them for who they were. This allowed me to help them focus on what they were good at and not worry about the rest. It felt great when I figured this out. It has also helped me to really enjoy supporting my kids since then.

Can you imagine what would happen if you enabled each person on your meeting team to focus on what he or she is really good at? How would that impact them? How would that impact your meetings? How would that impact your profits?

Sir Ken Robinson is a talented author and educator who brings out the best in people. In his brilliant 'Ted Talk' titled, "Do Schools Kill Creativity?"[22] Robinson asks us to encourage our kids for the 'A's that they get in school, and to stop worrying about the subjects in which they are getting 'D's. This wisdom has helped me to become a better father. And I believe that if you watch this video and learn this concept it will help you bring out the best in every person at your next team meeting.

Step 2E. Learn How To Fight

> "We find comfort among those who agree with us, growth among those who don't."[23]
>
> *Frank A. Clark*
> *Writer & Cartoonist*

If you want to get things done in a meeting you have to be able to disagree in a productive way and move on. But because so many people can't be real with each other they end up fighting and their meetings get bogged down. So here are a few suggestions to help you learn how to fight productively during meetings.

How Do We Fight Right Now?

You can begin to understand your meeting fight style by asking your team questions like:

- How do we deal with conflict?
- How do we feel about the way that we disagree?
- Is the way we disagree helping or hurting our profitability?

Create A Fight Style Inventory

Are you too nice? Too aggressive? How do you fight?

As a proud Canadian, I love hockey and maple syrup. I also love being polite, which is a great when I wear the maple leaf on my backpack as I travel through Europe, but it's brutal when I'm a participant in a team meeting.

Being too polite is a meeting killer because:

- It hides what people are really thinking
- Important discussions are avoided

Overly polite meeting warning signs include:

- "I didn't want to rock the boat"
- "I had to save face"
- "I always say yes"

Being too aggressive is a meeting killer because:

- It breaks trust
- It forces people to hide what they think and feel
- The meeting will be dominated by one or two aggressive people

Overly aggressive meeting warning signs include:

- "I crushed that guy"
- "I'm always right"
- "Screw you"

Once you understand how you fight, the next step is to figure out whether or not you want to do anything about it.

Figure Out 'Why' It's Worth Disagreeing

If you're going to ask your team to break a few eggs to make an awesome meeting omelet, it will be worth figuring 'why' you should learn to productively disagree. For example, if you are dealing with an important issue it may be critical to hear all points of view during a meeting so that you can make the most effective decision. If you understand this in advance, then you can warn everyone that this discussion may get heated, but that will be because people passionately believe in their own point of view. This type of preparation will help you build the right level of trust during the meeting in order to allow everyone to fully express themselves.

Learn How To Fight So You Can Really Get Along

Healthy disagreements during team meetings are great for business because:

- Your team won't allow a bad idea to make it out of the meeting room
- Your team will know that it's a good thing to speak up
- People will feel more confident to put their outlandish ideas forward, which will lead to more innovative outcomes
- Learning how to disagree effectively in a meeting will positively influence how you treat each other outside of the meeting
- Your team won't put up with the status quo
- Your team will support the winner and the loser of a fight in a productive way
- Your team will gain a competitive edge over your competition

Basic Rules of Meeting Fight Club

The first rule of Fight-Club-For-Team-Meetings is that you DO talk about fight club. Unlike how they kept fighting a secret in the 1999 movie *Fight Club*[24], it is crucial to be transparent about how you will productively handle disagreements. One way to do this is to develop a 'Meeting Fight Guideline' with each other and stick to it.

Meeting Fight Guideline Example

For example, you may all agree that in order to fight effectively during meetings you will:

- Make any disagreement about the issue, not about the people
- Be honest
- Know that it is OK to say 'No'
- Have one person talk at a time
- Set aside the right amount of time for each point
- Know when to 'parking lot' (set aside) an idea and then make sure you address it later
- Control levels and tones of voice
- Stop the discussion if it gets personal
- Step out of the room if someone gets angry
- Admit when you're wrong
- Ensure that once a decision is made that you and the entire team support it and move on

Tip: Check out 'Worksheet #3' in the Appendix of this guide to get a blank copy of the 'Meeting Fight Guideline'

Professional Meeting Facilitators Can Help You Learn How to Disagree

If your team can't figure out how to fight productively then you may want to bring in a Professional Meeting Facilitator. Based on my own experience, here are some of the benefits that you can expect when you hire a facilitator:

- Facilitators are objective and have no history with your team, so they can help you say what needs to be said

- They will help you to focus on issues and not on personalities
- Strategic facilitators can link how you fight during your meeting back to your overall strategic plan which will demonstrate whether or not the disagreement is worthwhile
- They can respectfully limit discussion time
- Facilitators can model 'fight moderation' behaviour from which the current meeting leader can learn from

Team Meeting Mentors

If you don't want to bring in an outside facilitator then perhaps you can find a meeting mentor within your own organization. This person will have a proven reputation for running effective meetings. For example, Business Networking International (BNI)[25] assigns 'Ambassadors' to work with various leadership teams throughout their organization. These experienced Ambassadors are able to guide any leadership team through its toughest challenges. This approach is one of the key reasons that Business Networking International's meetings are among the most effective in the world.

Is there anyone in your organization who is already an effective facilitator? Could that person be assigned to teach productive fighting skills to meeting teams throughout your organization? If you developed a reputation for being able to productively disagree during meetings, how would this impact your overall ability to recruit and retain the best people?

Step 2F. How To Celebrate Getting Real With Your Team

Many people work hard at fixing problems in meetings. Then, when they're done, they move on to the next problem. They don't stop to celebrate their success. Sometimes this is because they don't want to, or maybe they don't know how.

When I worked as a corporate manager I often praised individuals during team meetings when they had done something well. But that was about as far as I went when it came to celebrating. Looking back, it's clear that our department didn't celebrate more often because I wasn't very good at it. I would also bring up a lot of typical excuses, such as, 'the company can't afford to pay for a staff lunch so we can't do anything this year', and then not make any real effort to find an alternative. If I could go back now and speak to 'old me' I would ask him to learn how to celebrate with his staff more often in order to boost morale and productivity.

How do you celebrate wins in your team meetings?

Excuses To Not Celebrate

- There's no budget for celebrating this year
- We're all too busy
- We're just not very good at celebrating
- It's too much extra work to put together a celebration

Ways To Celebrate On A Tight Budget

- Start by asking your team for celebration suggestions
- Learn how to look each other in the eye and honestly say 'thank-you'
- Acknowledge your meeting team during the company

barbecue
- Have a potluck lunch before your next meeting
- The meeting leader can send handwritten thank-you cards to each team member
- Praise people directly through Social Media channels such as LinkedIn, Twitter, Facebook and Pinterest
- Get a group portrait of the meeting team done and put it on the meeting room wall
- Acknowledge team accomplishments in the staff newsletter
- Have someone who benefits from your work write a testimonial letter, and then get him or her to read it out loud at your next team meeting. This works especially well for customer service and non-profit board meetings.

Ways To Celebrate With Money $

- Measure meeting outcomes and tie them to year-end bonuses
- Give time off for outstanding performance during meetings
- Give gift cards for meals, travel, and entertainment
- As a team, you can choose a charity that you want to support and then, instead of doing your regular meeting, you can use the time to volunteer for that charity
- Have fun at off-site events like paintball, bowling, golf, and softball
- Take the whole team and their families on a vacation

Don't Wait To Celebrate

My dad died from a heart attack when I was 16. My mom died from lung cancer when I was 24. Do I wish I'd celebrated more with them? Yes. Do I wish I'd taken better care of my staff when I was a corporate manager? Yes. As a Professional Meeting Facilitator do I now make sure that my clients include celebration as part of every engagement? Yes.

So no. You're not too busy. And yes, you can figure out the most appropriate way to celebrate with your meeting team. Can you imagine how much a sincere celebration would help you to get real with your team? And when you do get real with each other you can expect more smiles and laughter, in addition to having more profitable meetings.

Step 2G. Invest Real Dollars To Grow Your Team

Does your organization invest in its people? Do you say that you invest in people and then don't follow through? For example, how would your company benefit if your team meeting leader was also an excellent facilitator? If you sent that team meeting leader for facilitation training would you consider that a cost or an investment? Ensuring that everyone on your team has the ability to contribute effectively in all of your meetings will help you improve the overall productivity and profitability of your organization. So if you truly want to get the most out of your team, then demonstrate your commitment by investing real dollars in its development.

Step 2: Conclusion

"A job worth doing is worth doing together."[26]

Author Unknown

The key ingredient for getting real with your team is trust. If you can't trust each other during a meeting then you are hurting your profitability. If you do trust each other, then the sky is the limit when it comes to how productive your meeting team can become. In order to deepen trust, you have to listen effectively and take responsibility for being heard. You also need to do what you say you are going to do. If you want to be known for using people's time wisely, then you should make your POINT with passion and clarity. If you can't trust someone, then that individual should be removed from your team. And if you truly want a teammate to grow his or her skills, then demonstrate your commitment by investing real dollars in getting that person

the proper training resources that he or she requires. If you need help getting real with your team, then work with a meeting mentor or hire a Professional Meeting Facilitator. Most important of all, celebrate.

And in the end, getting real with each other is an investment that will not only improve your meetings, it will also help your company grow its bottom line.

So what are you waiting for?

Step 2: Get Real With Your Team Checklist √

1. Write down a compelling list of reasons about 'why' it is important to get real with your meeting team
2. Rank your current meeting team meeting behaviour and then determine what you want you new team meeting behavior score to be. This will start you on the path to improvement
3. Build trust with each other by really understanding

each person on the meeting team, listening and being heard effectively, and supporting each person for his or her strengths

4.   Build a Meeting Team Traits Inventory
5.   Learn how to make a great P-O-I-N-T
6.   Learn how to fight
7.   Work with a meeting mentor or hire a Professional Meeting Facilitator
8.   Invest actual money and time to help your team get the right training that it needs to learn how to trust each other deeply
9.   Plan how to celebrate each time you deepen your team trust level
10. Show the owners how getting real with each other helps the company make more money

Tip: Check out Step 8 in this guide to find more awesome resources that will help you 'Get Real With Your Team'

Up Next

In "Step 3: Know Your Total Meeting Cost $" you'll find out how being accountable for the true costs of your meetings can improve profitability.

5

Step 3: Know Your Total Meeting Cost

Meetings Cost $ Millions

After 25 years in business, I have run or participated in over 2000 meetings. If it cost an average of $1,000 per meeting to pay everyone involved, then the total cost of all those meetings combined is well over $2 million! Did those meetings produce more than $2 million worth of value? Honestly, I couldn't say either way. That's because I never tracked the costs and outcomes of all of those meetings. These days, when I work as a Professional Meeting Facilitator I do track the impact of meetings and I am confident that the return on investment for running a great meeting can be about 10X or more when you account for both the real dollar value as well as overall productivity improvements for any organization.

How many meetings have you been in? How much did it cost you and your organization to conduct those meetings? How profitable were they?

"What's measured improves."[27]

Peter F. Drucker, Writer, Consultant

Know Your Total Meeting Cost Per Hour

When most organizations do their accounting they measure the cost of inventory, staff, overhead, and marketing, among other factors. But is there a line item for meetings? Not likely.

So how do you know if your meetings are worthwhile?

One way to figure this out is to actually measure the total cost-per-hour of your next meeting like this:

$ Wages per hour + $ Meeting Space Cost + $ Refreshments = $ Total Meeting Cost per hour

Example 1: 'Weekly Staff Meeting'

+ $ Wages for 6 people = $1,000 per hour
+ $ Room Rental, Heat, Audio/Visual Equipment = $200 per hour
+ $ Muffins/Bagels/Coffee = $25
= $ A Total Meeting Cost of $1,225 for one hour!

Example 2: 'Annual Corporate Board Meeting In Hawaii'

+ $ Wages for 6 people = $10,000 per hour
+ $ Room Rental, Heat, Audio/Visual Equipment = $1,000 per hour
+ $ Lunch, wine, cigars = $2,000
= $ A Total Meeting Cost of $13,000 for one hour!

Tip: Check out 'Worksheet #4' in the Appendix of this guide to get a blank copy of the 'Total Meeting Cost Per Hour'

Make It Count

Once you understand the actual hourly cost of your meeting then you can assess if it was worth having or not. For example, let's say you discussed a specific project at your weekly staff meeting. You know that the project generated a profit of $100,000 and you also know that the weekly staff meeting cost $1,000 to run. Now you can begin to assess how much the weekly staff meeting influenced that project profitability by asking questions like:

- Did the 'light bulb moment' that made that project so profitable happen during the weekly staff meeting?
- Were the right people with the right skills to advance the project at that meeting? Could we have earned more if we had more experts?
- If that project was so successful should we dedicate more of the weekly staff meeting time to future projects like it?

It is unlikely that you will come up with an exact dollar figure about how that weekly staff meeting connected to that project's profitability. Nevertheless, this exercise will help you think more clearly about who should be in your next meeting and what his or her likelihood of success will be in relation to specific projects. It's also an effective way to connect what is happening in your meetings to your strategic objectives.

Know Your Total Meeting Cost Per Year

If your weekly staff meeting costs $1,000, then overall it will cost your organization around $50,000 per year. Is having a weekly staff meeting the best investment of $50,000 a year for your company? Is it better than buying a new piece of equipment? Is it better than paying for outside contractors? These are the types of 'Opportunity Cost' questions that you should be asking in order to make your next meeting as profitable as possible.

Opportunity Cost Explained

I define Opportunity Cost as 'the difference between what you choose and what you could have chosen.' For example, if you choose to talk about the office summer barbeque for one hour during the weekly staff meeting, then you lost the opportunity to talk about how to improve sales during that hour.

If you want to improve the profitability of your meetings you need to know the Opportunity Cost of what you choose to do versus what you could have done. For example, imagine that you have a $1000-per-hour lawyer sitting in a meeting in which everyone is talking about the latest cat videos. Would that be a good use of that lawyer's time?

When you prepare the agenda for your next meeting, write down a comparison of what you will probably talk about versus what you should be talking about. Then your meeting facilitator can use this list to make sure that you stay on track, as in:

What we will probably talk about:

- Sales results
- The summer staff barbeque gluten-free hot dog issue
- Cute cat videos

What we should talk about:

- Additional training to help sales staff achieve monthly targets
- Cash flow problems
- How to retain key staff

Looking Beyond The Dollars $

Not every organization measures profits in terms of cash. Along with lost dollars another brutal cost of bad meetings is lost time.

For example, in the Harvard Business Review article titled "This Weekly Meeting Took Up To 300,000 Hours Per Year,"[28] Michael C. Mankins uncovers how one large company spent 300,000 hours supporting one ongoing Executive Committee meeting.

Non-profit board meetings can be another type of meeting where time is not used well. This is often because people are too friendly or they don't have the right skill set to run an effective meeting. The result is that a lot of precious volunteer hours get burned up. If this happens it is usually followed by some polite (or impolite) volunteer resignations.

Can your non-profit board afford volunteer turnover? Imagine spending all those recruiting hours to find an experienced professional like an Accountant, and then finding out that the Accountant quit because the board meetings were not well run.

If you knew the total cost per hour of your next non-profit board meeting, how would that affect your meeting preparation? What impact would holding an effective board meeting have on volunteer recruiting and retention? Here is an example to get you started:

Example: 'Monthly Non-Profit Board Meeting'

+ $ Wages for 12 people = $2,200 per hour
+ $ Room Rental, Heat, Audio/Visual Equipment = $200 per hour
+ $ Refreshments = $50
= $ A Total Meeting Cost of $2,450 for one hour!

Step 3: Conclusion

According to BusinessInsider.com the cost of unproductive meetings is more than $37 Billion[29] per year in the United States alone! Globally that means that bad meetings could be costing us over $1 trillion a year!

I believe that bad meetings are like smoking. We get hooked early and it's hard to quit. But now is the time to break our addiction to bad meetings!

To do this you have to answer these questions:

- What type of meeting would we have if we understood exactly how much it costs to put it on?
- What will happen if we connect what we're doing in our meetings with our profitability?
- What is the Opportunity Cost of holding our next meeting? Should we be doing something else instead?

Answering these types of questions will help you turn your meetings into a competitive advantage that will help your company improve its profitability.

Step 3: Know Your Total Meeting Cost $ Checklist √

1. Do we understand the current overall cost of our meetings?
2. How can we connect the cost of our meetings to our overall profitability?
3. How can we account for non-dollar factors such as time and staff morale when we measure our meeting costs?
4. How important is it for us to have a great facilitator in each one of our meetings?
5. Should we pay to train our current meeting leader to become a more effective facilitator?
6. Should we hire a Professional Meeting Facilitator to improve our meetings right now?
7. What is the Opportunity Cost of holding our meetings? Should we be investing our time in something else?
8. How can we turn our meetings into a competitive advantage?
9. How will we celebrate when we succeed?
10. How can we demonstrate that investing the right amount of time and money into our meetings will make our organization stronger?

Tip: Check out Step 8 in this guide to find more awesome resources that will help you to actually 'Know Your Total Meeting Cost $'

Up Next

In 'Step 4: Get A Great Facilitator' you'll find out how to make sure that the best-of-the-best are leading your meetings.

6

Step 4: Get A Great Facilitator

Who Is Leading Your Meetings?

Do your current meeting leaders make your gatherings productive, fun and engaging? Or do they arrive late, pick favourites and laugh at their own jokes? Awesome meetings start with great facilitators. So if your current meeting leaders are up for it, here are a few ways to help them learn how to become more effective:

- You can help your current meeting leader to become a better facilitator by getting that person the right level of training
- You can also help your leader find a mentor who really understands group facilitation
- In addition, you could hire a Professional Meeting Facilitator to help your current leader learn how to run more productive meetings

Another way to help your meeting leader grow is to take a snapshot of his or her current facilitation ability, and then compare that to the level that you would like him or her to achieve.

Rate The Competency Level Of Your Current Meeting Facilitator

Rate the competency level of your current meeting facilitator on a scale of 1-10.

1-4/10 - A Low Score

Meeting Facilitator Competencies Include:

- Untrustworthy
- Unprepared
- Bad listener
- Talks too much
- Doesn't spark new ideas
- People hate the meetings
- Meeting results are poor

5-8/10 - An Average Score

Meeting Facilitator Competencies Include:

- Trustworthy
- Prepares agenda in advance
- Listens well
- Good time manager
- People like the meetings
- Meeting results are adequate

9-10/10 - Outstanding Score

Meeting Facilitator Competencies Include:

- Confident, firm and passionate
- Listens deeply
- Brings out the best in everyone
- Loves to laugh
- Humble and admits mistakes
- Links the results of the meeting to your organization strategy
- Able to quickly read the mood of everyone during the meeting and adjust accordingly
- Helps people disagree in a highly productive and respectful way
- Ensures that each person commits to at least one action item before he or she leaves the room
- People love being in the meeting
- The meetings are highly productive and profitable

Write your current meeting facilitator competency score here:

_____ / 10

Write what you want your meeting facilitator competency score to be here:

_____ / 10

Closing Your Meeting Leader's Facilitation Skills Gap

Now that you know your current meeting leader's

competency level, here are a few suggestions to help improve his or her facilitation abilities.

Facilitation Training Options

1. The International Association of Facilitators (IAF) is a participatory organization with representation in over 65 countries. The IAF believes, "Good facilitation can change the way people think and act, and ultimately support them to positively change the world around them."[31]

2. The Masterful Facilitation Institute "Exists to build your confidence and skills as an effective facilitator so you can design and facilitate great meetings, group sessions and workshops - every time, for any purpose."[32]

3. Your local University, College or Polytechnic will likely offer facilitation training courses. For example, Simon Fraser University in British Columbia, Canada, offers a course called "Effective Group Facilitation"[33] through their Continuing Studies department

4. Your local business association should be able to help you find more facilitation training options

5. You could also find a meeting mentor or hire a Professional Meeting Facilitator to coach your current meeting leader

What Can You Do With A Bad Meeting Leader?

Is your current meeting leader resistant to change? If he or she is, and your meetings aren't improving, then it's time to explore all options, including:

- Can he or she 'get real with themselves' by working through Step 1 in this guide?
- Can someone else lead the meeting?
- Can the leader be removed from the meeting?
- If this bad meeting leader stays, can the organization afford more unproductive meetings?
- Will you lose your best employees or volunteers if the bad meetings continue?

Set The Meeting Leader Up For Training Success

Putting a proper training program in place can help your current meeting leader to vastly improve his or her facilitation skills. But too often this type of training is treated as 'extra,' which means that your leader has to add it to his or her already ridiculous pile of duties. Here are a few suggestions to help you create a successful training program:

- Invest the proper amount of money to get the best facilitation training you can afford
- Find a style of training that suits your meeting leader
- Set out clear expectations for the training. For example, you can establish clear start and end dates as well as the outcomes you expect from the leader after that person completes the facilitation training
- Free up the leader's schedule so he or she can focus on the training, which may include finding someone to backfill for the leader on specific projects
- Encourage the leader and give that individual feedback as he or she goes through this facilitation training process

"You are your greatest asset. Put your time,
effort and money into training, grooming and en-
couraging your greatest asset."[34]

Tom Hopkins, Author

Work With A Meeting Mentor

Another way to inspire your current meeting leader is to
find them a suitable mentor. The following steps will help
you begin this process:

1. You can start by searching within your own organiza-
    tion or by asking 'friends' of your organization, and if
    you can't find a mentor within this group then you
    can contact relevant professional associations and
    colleges to get a referral
2. Once you have identified a potential mentor you
    should get in touch with that person to find out his or
    her interest level
3. You should also explain the high stakes involved, as
    in, "If our current meeting leader doesn't improve
    then he or she will be removed from the meeting"
4. Then you can create a clear 'road map' for the men-
    torship commitment. For example, you could ask the
    mentor to work one-on-one with the meeting leader
    for two consecutive sessions
5. Then you could ask the mentor to sit in on the next
    meeting as an observer
6. Afterwards, the mentor could meet with your meeting
    leader to give feedback
7. You could then follow up by measuring whether or
    not your current meeting leader has improved
8. Then you can work with the mentor and the meeting

leader to figure out the next steps

"A friend will tell you what you want to hear. A mentor will tell you what you need to hear to change."[35]

John Di Lemme, Strategic Business Coach

Hire A Professional Facilitator To Help Your Meeting Leader

Not only can a Professional Meeting Facilitator help you make your meetings more productive and profitable, the facilitator can also serve as a role model for your current leader. Here is a list of positive behaviours that you should expect to learn from a Professional Meeting Facilitator:

- Their attitude should be enthusiastic and firm
- They should be honest and transparent
- They should be able to help everyone fully express themselves
- They should make sure that everyone in the meeting is heard, including people who are usually quiet
- They should help you link what happens during the meeting to your organization's 'big picture'
- They should be excellent time managers
- They should be able to make people laugh and have fun

Facilitator Fit

When you hire a Professional Meeting Facilitator you want to make sure that he or she has a style that will bring out the best in everyone at your meeting. Here are some questions you can ask before you hire a facilitator:

- How would you describe your approach to facilitation?
- How do you keep the meeting focused on issues instead of people?
- How do you build trust during a meeting?
- Describe the best meeting facilitation you have ever done
- How do you deal with confidentiality, especially around trade secrets and other sensitive information that will be brought up during the meeting?
- Will you sign a non-disclosure agreement?
- Do you have professional insurance including errors and omissions and commercial general liability insurance?
- Can you provide references from meetings that you have facilitated in the past?
- Can you submit a formal proposal about how you would approach this engagement?
- Can you provide an engagement contract?

Additional Facilitator Hiring Considerations May Include:

- Do you also need your Professional Meeting Facilitator to be a subject matter expert? If so, you may consider connecting with larger consulting firms to see if they have someone with facilitation skills who is also a subject matter expert. You may also want to get in touch with your industry association to see if they know of anyone with this double skill set
- Before you hire a Professional Meeting Facilitator, ask that person if you can assign someone to shadow him or her before, during and after the meeting. This will

allow the person from your organization to learn the facilitator's best practices. Then the person from your organization can teach those best practices to your people and you can grow the meeting facilitation capacity within your company. This will also help you avoid 'learned helplessness', which could occur if you continually hire outsiders to solve your meeting facilitation problems

The Opportunity Cost Of Facilitation Training

To decide whether or not you should pay for facilitation training for your current meeting leader you have to measure the Opportunity Cost. As you learned in Step 3 of this guide, Opportunity Cost is "the difference between what you choose and what you could have chosen." To help you figure out whether or not you should send your leader to a course, or have him or her work with a meeting mentor or a Professional Meeting Facilitator, here are a few key questions to consider:

- What will our meetings continue to be like if we don't invest in facilitation training for our current meeting leader?
- How much better could our meetings be if we do invest in facilitation training?

Facilitation Training Return On Investment

Facilitation training is only worthwhile if your current leader is a quick learner who can immediately apply new skills to make your meetings more profitable. And no matter which type of training you decide to invest in, you'll need to measure the outcome to determine whether or not the training was worth the cost. Here are a few suggestions to help you do this:

- Send a survey to your meeting team a month after your meeting leader has completed the facilitation training. In the survey you can ask the meeting team about how the meeting leader is running the meetings since they did the facilitation training
- Measure the actual profitability of your most recent meetings, and determine whether or not this is related to the performance of your meeting leader
- Send a survey to the meeting leader a month after he or she has completed the facilitation training to get input about whether or not it was worthwhile

My Professional Meeting Facilitation Approach

For your reference, here is a step-by-step explanation of my Professional Meeting Facilitation approach. Of course every facilitator will have his or her own style, but the fundamentals should be relatively the same.

1. **Define the scope of the engagement** - First, I meet with the clients and their key stakeholders well in advance of the meeting to:
   - Understand their overall strategic objectives

   - Clearly define what they want to achieve during the meeting
   - Get a true understanding of all the different people who will be attending the meeting
   - Establish the meeting return on investment the client is expecting for booking me as a facilitator

2. **Choose the meeting location** - Then I make sure that the meeting room has been selected, and I work with the client to discuss the room layout and inform the client about any technical requirements (projector, sound system, charts, pens, paper, etc.)

3. **Research and preparation** - Next, I prepare for the meeting by choosing appropriate exercises and information that will make the meeting successful

4. **Stay connected** - During this time I also connect frequently with the meeting leader and any other key stakeholders to make sure that I haven't missed any important details

5. **Set up early** - On the meeting day, I arrive early and set up the room with everything you need to have a successful meeting, including paper on the walls, pens, stickies, pads, paper and I also double-check all PowerPoint slides

6. **Greet each person** - When everyone arrives, I make contact with each person to establish a rapport and then I get each person to put his or her name on a card in front of where he or she is sitting

7. **Get introduced** - I ask the client to kick-off the meeting and introduce me as the facilitator. This clearly establishes me as the main person who will be running the meeting

8. **Establish credibility** - I introduce myself after the client kicks off the meeting. This establishes credibility, especially for people that I am meeting for the first time. For example I start every meeting off by letting people know that I:
   o Have facilitated, run or participated in more than 2000 meetings
   o Have over 25 years of work experience as a facilitator, consultant, manager, and employee

- o Earned a Master's Degree in Business Administration from the University of Alberta
- o Earned a Drama Degree from Queen's University, and I point out that this is why I take a people-centered approach to meeting facilitation
- o Earned Prosci Change Management Certification
- o I'm a Dad, husband, community volunteer and more

9. **Go over meeting details** - Then I bring focus to the meeting by introducing the agenda, requesting that those in attendance turn off their phones, telling them where they can find the washrooms, and asking if anybody has any questions or concerns

10. **Relevant self-introductions** - Then I have each person introduce themselves in a way that is relevant to the topic of the meeting. For example:
    - o If the purpose of the meeting is to innovate then I ask that each person tell the group a personal story about when they led a successful innovation
    - o If the meeting purpose is to get to know each other then I get each person tell the group something that nobody knows about him or her

11. **Go with the flow and keep it interesting** - During the meeting I follow a pre-determined plan but I always remain fluid to allow for additional relevant discussion, and I usually make sure to break up a large group meeting by having people work in small groups midway through

12. **Summarize frequently** - I summarize as often as possible during the meeting and keep the group on track

13. **Reinforcement** - I also provide ongoing clarification and support for people as they share their ideas
14. **Capture all good points** - When good points are made that are not related to the goal of the meeting, I record them and save the ideas for later. Facilitators often refer to this as putting the ideas in a 'parking lot,' so you can return to them afterwards
15. **Help people disagree productively** - I also embrace and nurture conflict, but when a disagreement occurs I make sure to keep the discussion based around the issue and not on the personalities
16. **Keep the energy up** - I often challenge the group when there is a dip in the energy in the room. This can be done by simply standing up and stretching, or it may involve digging deeply into their toughest issues
17. **Summarize and praise** - At the end of the meeting I do a thorough summary of ideas as well as point out the effective behaviours that the group exhibited
18. **Call to action** - I also look each individual in the eye and ask "What are you going to do when you leave the room?" and I make sure that each one of them states his or her full answer out loud so that everybody can hear what was said. This is a great way to create accountability
19. **Follow up** - I always follow up with the client to get feedback after a meeting

---

"Having gathered a group of smart and powerful people to consult on a potential new project, I was nervous; these were not people with time to waste. I put my trust in Gord to create a meeting that would make good use of the time they were spending in the room that day, and he did not disappoint. Somehow, he simultaneously fostered a relaxed and casual atmosphere while keeping us on topic and on schedule. He ushered us through an extremely productive and rewarding conversation but never gave us any feeling of being controlled or overly formal. Not only did we accomplish our objectives, several of my attendees commented to me afterwards on the quality of the meeting and the facilitation. I'm grateful to have had Gord in my corner that day.

Nadine Riopel
Facilitator and Community Organizer

Step 4: Conclusion

How much longer can you afford to have mediocre meetings? What would happen if you invested in your current meeting leader to help him or her become an awesome facilitator? Not only will your meetings improve but your team will become more motivated, and that will have a positive impact on your bottom line.

Step 4: Get A Great Facilitator Checklist √

1. Do an honest assessment of your meeting leader's current facilitation abilities, and then determine what facilitation competency level you want them to get to
2. Don't hesitate to remove an ineffective meeting leader
3. Get the right type of facilitation training to suit your meeting leader's style so he or she can be successful
4. Set a clear facilitation training schedule, and budget to have additional personnel available to backfill on

current projects that the meeting leader will no longer be able to finish because he or she is going to do facilitation training

5. Consider whether or not it is worth bringing in a meeting mentor or hiring a Professional Meeting Facilitator

6. Learn what to ask so that you can find the right meeting mentor or Professional Meeting Facilitator

7. Make the extra effort to learn as much as possible from meeting mentors and Professional Meeting Facilitators so that you can build up internal facilitation capacity and also avoid becoming overly dependent on outside help

8. Measure the return on investment for any type of facilitation training

9. Plan how to celebrate when your leader becomes an awesome meeting facilitator

10. Demonstrate why investing in the right meeting facilitator is great for business

Tip: Check out Step 8 in this guide to find more awesome resources that will help you and your team 'Get A Great Facilitator'

Up Next

In "Step 5: Link The Meeting To Your Strategy" you'll discover how to connect every meeting moment to your organization's 'big picture.'

7

Step 5: Link The Meeting To Your Strategy

Strategic Questions

After going through the first four steps in this guide you now understand how to get real with yourself, how to get real with your team, how to figure out your actual meeting costs, and how to ensure that you have an awesome meeting facilitator. Now it's time to link your meetings directly to your organization strategy. You can begin this process by asking:

- What is our strategy?
- What are our top three strategic objectives?
- Can everyone in our meeting clearly explain our top three strategic objectives?
- How does our strategy influence our meetings?
- How do our meetings influence our strategy?
- Do our meetings and strategy combine to make us more profitable?

'If you don't know where you are going, any road will get you there.'[36]

Lewis Carroll, Author

How NOT To Link Your Meetings To Your Strategy

When I worked as an employee I always did my job well, but if we were in a meeting and you had asked me "What are the company's top three strategic objectives?" I would have been stumped. Why? Honestly, I was pretty self-centered. WIIFM, as in What's-In-It-For-Me was the perspective that I had during meetings, which meant that I didn't pay much attention to details that didn't affect me. And it wasn't because the companies I worked for didn't have strategic objectives. In fact, I'm certain that all of those executive teams worked hard to develop complex, profitable strategic plans every year. And every year someone in their communications department would send out a condensed version of the new strategic plan via mass email, often in a new shape like a pyramid or a square. But by the time these strategic plans arrived in our inboxes, they didn't convey a lot of real meaning for workers on the front line.

One time I was a manager who had to tell his department about the new strategic plan. I remember feeling the pit in my stomach at the beginning of our weekly staff meeting as I began my pitch. It was a tough sell for a few reasons. My first thought was, 'How can I sell the big picture when I can't even get budget approval for the basic tools that my staff needs to do their jobs?' My next frustration was that I didn't have a method to immediately apply the elaborate strategic objectives contained within the plan. As a result, I did a lousy job of trying to get my staff to care about it. Looking back, I wish I had a better understanding about 'why' those strategic objectives were supposed to be important to my team. Knowing the 'why' might have helped me do a better job of connecting our meetings to the company's strategic plan.

My Strategic Inspiration

During that difficult meeting I did try one significant thing. I asked the staff to see if there was a way to translate specific parts of this strategic plan into plain language that we could all understand and use. For example, one of the strategic objectives implied that we should drive growth in the business-to-business market. We put that objective into our own words so that it sounded something like, 'we will continue to deliver excellent communications products that our clients will tell their clients about.' It was a small win during a very unsatisfying meeting. Looking back, I wish I had the ability to follow that effort through. But it was the right idea at the wrong time.

That bad meeting experience was one of the main inspirations for me to go back to school to do a Master's in Business Administration (MBA) at the age of forty-two. I earned that degree while working full-time, raising two kids, and being fortunate enough to have an incredibly supportive wife (thanks Tracy). I also earned that degree because I wanted to know how to actually link any company's strategic plan to every aspect of its operations, including meetings. So now, when I work as a Professional Meeting Facilitator, I am able to use all of my experience and training to help my clients connect every one of their meetings directly to their strategic plan.

Make Every Meeting Count

Because the pace of business moves so quickly, you have to make every meeting count. Linking your organization strategy to all of your meetings is a great way to do this.

> "Change is not a destination, just as "Hope" is not a strategy."[37]
>
> *Rudy Giuliani, Lawyer*
> *Former Mayor of New York City*

Start With The Right Questions And Resources

This book doesn't cover how to build an organization strategy. But here are some basic questions and an outline for you to refer to as you begin to connect your meetings to your strategic plan.

Strategic Planning Questions

- Where are we today?
- Where do we want to go?
- How are we going to get there?

Strategic Planning Outline

1. Vision
2. Mission
3. Core Values
4. Strategic Objectives and Goals
5. A Current Status Review, often based on a SWOT Analysis (Strengths, Weaknesses, Opportunities & Threats)
6. Financing Needs
7. Talent Needs
8. Resource Requirements

9. Marketing Approach
10. Key Performance Indicators

And if you need help with your strategic plan, please get in touch with me at gord@createawesomemeetings.com

How To Link Your Strategic Plan To Your Meeting

In the same way that a camera can zoom in or zoom out, you should be able to zoom in to specific details during your meeting and then zoom out so you can connect them to your strategic plan. The following steps will help you zoom in and zoom out with ease:

- Step 5A. The Strategic Meeting Check-In
- Step 5B. Use Strategic Language That Everyone Understands
- Step 5C. Create Your Own Strategic Story

Step 5A. The Strategic Meeting Check-In

To see if you are actually connecting each meeting moment to your strategic plan you can do a Strategic Meeting Check-In once or twice during each meeting. For example, after you have finished discussing a specific topic, summarize it and then ask the group to tell you which part of your strategic plan will benefit. Here are a couple of examples to get you started:

EXAMPLE 1 - Marketing Growth

Meeting Moment: We just finished discussing a direct mail marketing campaign that will help us reach a new customer segment

Strategic Objective: Sell aggressively into new niche markets

How This Meeting Moment Benefits Our Strategy: By doing the direct mail marketing campaign and measuring the results we can see if this action helps us reach a new set of customers. And if it doesn't, then we can quickly test an alternative marketing tactic that will help us sell more aggressively into niche markets

EXAMPLE 2 - Talent Retention

Meeting Moment: We just discussed how to pay for additional training for a talented manager

Strategic Objective: Attract and retain the best talent

How This Meeting Moment Benefits Our Strategy: Our top employee feels grateful for the opportunity to get training and upgrade her skills. The company will benefit when she completes the training because she will become a more effective manager who will communicate more clearly with her direct reports. Doing all we can to make her happy in her job reflects our key strategic objective of doing everything possible to attract and retain the best talent in our industry

Follow Up

One of the best ways to reinforce a Strategic Meeting Check-In during a meeting is to follow up on it. For example, let's say that the direct mail campaign actually helped you acquire a new customer. At your next meeting you could note that the Strategic Meeting Check-In that you did during your last meeting was one of the key steps that got you this win. This approach will reinforce how useful Strategic Meeting Check-Ins can be.

To make this approach even more successful you should track the information that you gather during and after a Strategic Meeting Check-In. This can be done by:

- Choosing an appropriate database solution that everybody can access and put information into
- Being aware that information will only be useful if the person who is inputting it is consistent and able to distribute the information in a way that people will read it
- Not leaving your information on sticky notes, or sitting in a document on one person's computer
- Assigning someone other than the meeting leader to input the information and track the results
- Summarizing the Strategic Meeting Check-In data and using it to develop your next strategic plan
- Reading Step 9 in this book and following up F-A-S-T

Step 5B. Use Strategic Language That Everyone Understands

Is it easy to explain your strategic plan? What would happen if you translated the most important parts of your strategic plan into plain language that could be used by everyone in your next meeting?

Example 1 - Vision Statement Translation

What if your Vision Statement was, "Be the #1 service provider for the next 100 years." You could translate that into, "We will ask every customer and their kids for real feedback so that we can keep their whole family as a client for many generations to come."

Example 2 - Mission Statement Translation

What if your Mission Statement was, "We will be the most cost-effective manufacturer in our industry." Your meeting team might translate this into, "We will report accurate manufacturing costs during every weekly meeting and if they rise too much we will figure out the problem and take corrective action immediately, and we won't bury our heads in the sand and hope the problem goes away."

Creating strategic language that everybody understands will improve communication. It will also allow your staff to take a deeper ownership stake in the company's strategic plan, which will improve meeting productivity and overall profitability.

Step 5C. Create Your Own Strategic Story

Everybody loves a good story. What would happen if you could turn your strategic plan into a great story that your staff loves? To get you started, here is an example of how you might use a 'Soap Opera' storyline.

Strategic Story 'Soap Opera' Example

Cast of Characters

You can start by assembling a great cast of characters that turn the most important parts of your strategic plan into references that everyone can relate to. For example:

- **Vision = Dad**, who helps us imagine what we could become
- **Mission = Mom**, who is awesome at keeping the

whole family on track and doesn't put up with any crap
- **Objectives = Big Brother**, who takes direction from Mom and Dad and then watches over the family to make sure that things get done
- **Goals = Little Sister**, who doesn't always like listening to her older brother but she makes sure he looks good for Mom and Dad
- **Customer = Grandma**, a demanding old lady who is almost impossible to please, but when we do satisfy her and she cracks that false tooth smile it makes it all worthwhile, and we all make a lot of money

Then, instead of referring to typical strategic planning words like Vision, Mission and Goals, you can refer to the Cast of Characters above when talking about a problem.

Now you can imagine a typical problem that might be discussed during a meeting. For example, let's say your salesperson missed a delivery. Now he or she has to explain what happened to the boss.

Story: The Missed Delivery And The Angry Customer

Boss: "Why did you miss that delivery deadline? Big Brother is mad."

Salesperson: "Little Sister was asking for too much and so I forgot to talk to Grandma."

Boss: "Mom and Dad are not happy about this. So what can we do?"

Salesperson: "I'll call Grandma myself and explain what happened and go above and beyond to do everything we can to keep her in the family."

Boss: "Before the next meeting?"
Salesperson: "Yes."

To customize this approach there are many characters you could choose from, like:

- The players on your favourite sports team
- Your favourite superheroes
- The musicians in an orchestra
- Your favourite cartoon characters

This playful approach is a great way to help you connect your strategy to the most important moments in your next meeting.

Step 5: Conclusion

"A goal without a plan is just a wish."[38]

Antoine de Saint-Exupéry, Author

How powerful would your next meeting be if it moved your strategic plan forward? What if everyone in your meeting understood your strategic objectives, and then they went above and beyond to make them happen? And like the canary in the coalmine checking for dangerous gases, testing your strategy in each meeting will give you a strong indication about how your organization is performing overall. Then you won't have to wait for the annual strategic review to make adjustments. So if you want to turn your meetings into a competitive advantage, then it's time to connect each meeting moment to your organization strategy.

Step 5: Link The Meeting To Your Strategy Checklist √

1. Can everybody in our meeting easily describe our top 3 strategic objectives?
2. Are we connecting each moment in our meeting to our strategy?
3. Are we making every meeting moment count?
4. When will we do the first Strategic Meeting Check-In at our next meeting?
5. How can we turn our strategic plan into plain language that everyone can use?
6. What is our strategic story?
7. How do we track the data that we gather during Strategic Meeting Check-Ins?
8. How do we measure Strategic Meeting Check-Ins?
9. Once we have successfully executed three Strategic Meeting Check-Ins, how are we going to celebrate?
10. How can we demonstrate that Strategic Meeting Check-Ins help us make more money?

Tip: Check out Step 8 in this guide to find more awesome resources that will help you and your team 'Link The Meeting To Your Strategy'

Up Next

In "The Ultimate Meeting Moment" you'll find out how connecting Step 1 + Step 2 + Step 5 in this guide can help you make your meetings exceptionally profitable.

8

The Ultimate Meeting Moment

I believe that you should be able to stop any meeting at any moment and be able to connect that moment directly to your strategic plan. Ideally, this means that every moment of your next meeting should be moving your organization strategy forward.

Give It A Try

Try this during your next meeting:

- Pick an appropriate moment during your meeting
- Stop
- Ask your team, "Is what we're doing right now moving our organization strategy forward?"

If your team can answer confidently and quickly then you're having a great meeting. But if nobody answers, or worse, they don't know what your strategic objectives are, then you're in a bad meeting. At that point, I would suggest you stop the discussion and use the rest of the time to clarify your strategic objectives and connect them to what you're doing. Because if you can't articulate how what you are doing in the meeting is helping your strategy, then you have a big problem. And the canary in your coal mine just died.

The Ultimate Meeting Moment

The Ultimate Meeting Moment measures how you, your team and your strategy combine during a meeting. It's based on this formula:

Real Me + Real Team + Real Strategy = The Ultimate Meeting Moment

- Real Me (Step 1) - Each person is self-aware and confident
- Real Team (Step 2) - You all trust each other
- Real Strategy (Step 5) - Everyone understands why they are in the meeting and how their actions in that moment will move the organization strategy forward

Does the possibility of doing this well give you goose bumps? Can you imagine how profitable your meetings will become when you put this process into action?

Putting The Ultimate Meeting Moment Formula Into Action

1. Stop The Meeting And Ask The Question

- Pick an appropriate moment during your meeting
- Stop
- Ask your team, "Is what we are doing right now moving our organization strategy forward?"

2. Rate The 3 Key Components Of That Ultimate Meeting Moment

Rate everyone's Ultimate Meeting Moment performance from 1-10 based on this scale:

1-4/10 - A Low Score

'Real Me' Behaviours Include:

- Checking your phone
- Slouching and folding your arms
- Not answering the meeting leader

'Real Team' Behaviours Include:

- Talking for too long about what you did on the weekend
- Watching cat videos together
- Being overly sarcastic

'Real Strategy' Behaviours Include:

- Nobody knows what your top 3 strategic objectives are
- Nobody can state your Vision and Mission
- Nobody cares about your organization strategy

5-8/10 - An Average Score

'Real Me' Behaviours Include:

- You are nice during the meeting
- You are helpful to your team members
- You have at least one positive thing to say about each member of your meeting team

'Real Team' Behaviours Include:

- Basic level of trust
- Everybody is nice and follows the agenda
- There may be some conflicts but nobody talks about them

'Real Strategy' Behaviours Include:

- Some people can say what your top 3 strategic objectives are
- People understand your Vision and Mission but they don't all express it in the same way
- People care about your organization strategy

9-10/10 - Outstanding Score

'Real Me' Behaviours Include:

- You are fully self-aware of your good/bad behaviours
- You choose how you want to act during the meeting
- You confidently share your best ideas

'Real Team' Behaviours Include:

- There is a high level of trust and constructive conflicts are welcomed
- Innovative ideas happen often
- People encourage each other and laugh out loud

'Real Strategy' Behaviours Include:

- Any person in your meeting can easily explain what

your top 3 strategic objectives are
- Each person passionately connects to your Vision and Mission
- Each person takes responsibility for making sure that everything he or she does is moving your organization strategy forward so you can all win

3. Apply the Ultimate Meeting Moment formula

Real Me + Real Team + Real strategy = The Ultimate Meeting Moment

4. Write your Ultimate Meeting Moment score here:

_____ / 10

5. Write what you want your Ultimate Meeting Moment score to become here:

_____ / 10

The Ultimate Meeting Moment Formula Summary

1. Stop the meeting and ask the question
2. Rate everyone's Ultimate Meeting Moment performance
3. Apply the Ultimate Meeting Moment Formula
4. Record your current Ultimate Meeting Moment Score
5. Record what you want your Ultimate Meeting Moment score to be

Take Action!

Achieving 'The Ultimate Meeting Moment' is challenging but worth it. So here are a few suggestions to get you started:

- Give yourself the proper amount of time to work through Steps 1, 2 and 5 in this guide and then put them into action!
- Learn from companies that do this well. For example, when Jack Welch was CEO of General Electric in the 1980s, he stated that any division within General Electric should be number 1 or 2 in their industry.[39] This clear strategic objective could be measured and understood by anyone having a meeting at GE during that time
- Gather the data - When you stop your meeting and discuss whether or not it is helping your strategy, you have to record the key points and follow up on them. It is the only way to make your team accountable. Then, during your next meeting you can revisit the key points to see whether or not you're making progress

Achieving 'The Ultimate Meeting Moment' will not only improve your company's profits, but it will make an enormous difference in your overall meeting team satisfaction level.

So what are you waiting for?

Up Next

In "Step 6: Build A Blockbuster Agenda" you'll get all the tools you need to create an awesome agenda that will motivate your staff to create the most productive meetings you've ever had!

9

Step 6: Build A Blockbuster A-G-E-N-D-A

Create An Awesome Story

Imagine what would happen if every meeting you attended was as exciting as your favourite Hollywood blockbuster movie?

For example, *The Lion King* has earned over $11 Billion USD from box office, stage adaptation and merchandising revenues[40]. But before all that money poured in, they had to start with a great story, and a great story starts with a great script.

What if every one of your meetings had a great script? And what I mean by great script is a great meeting agenda, complete with a memorable story, passionate characters and a financial return that is beyond your expectations. Just like *The Lion King.*

Re-Thinking The Agenda

Oh the poor little meeting agenda. Just like a Hollywood blockbuster movie that flops at the box office, the meeting agenda is usually ignored and forgotten. Why?

- Because someone has to prepare it, and we rarely build agenda preparation time into our work days
- A strong agenda should have input from multiple people, which usually takes too much time away from our other work
- Most often the agendas are not followed during meetings anyway, so whoever prepared the agenda gets discouraged and then puts very little effort into preparing the agenda for the next meeting

But if you don't put any effort into preparing your agenda then you can expect your next meeting to be a flop.

Make Your Next Meeting Agenda A Blockbuster

Hollywood blockbusters have a formula for their scripts that go something like this:

- **Beginning** - Something big happens to draw us into the movie. Like when sharks fall from the sky or aliens eat New York
- **Middle** - There is a little victory and then a big setback. Like when a small band of heroes fight a million ugly guys from middle earth and the main character with the fuzzy feet gets fatally stabbed in the chest
- **End** - The Hero overcomes the setback and then there is a big climax and everything is resolved!

Compare that Hollywood blockbuster story approach with this typical agenda outline:

1. Roll call
2. Approve previous meeting minutes
3. State goal of the meeting

4. Old business discussion
5. New business discussion
6. Book the next meeting
7. Adjourn

If this agenda outline were turned into a Hollywood blockbuster movie, would you want to go see it? Neither would I. So how can you prepare a meeting agenda that will be as inspired as the script for *Star Wars* or *Avatar*?

Write With Your Audience In Mind

Great Hollywood writers really understand their audience. Great business people really understand their customers. So to be a great business-meeting leader you should treat every person in your next meeting like they were your best customers. And just like a Hollywood writer wants to delight the audience, you should prepare a meeting agenda that will delight your best customers, because:

- A great meeting agenda can help you motivate your meeting team and turn them into raving fans who will go above and beyond to achieve your company's goals
- You know that your best customers are busy and their time is valuable, so you should write a concise meeting agenda that respects your meeting team's time
- You know that your best customer has a short attention span, which is no different than your staff, so you can customize your meeting agenda to be clear and concise
- If you think about it, how much do you actually remember after you watch your favourite movie? If you

keep this in mind then you can write as many memorable items into your meeting agenda as possible in
order to create the highest retention possible
amongst your meeting team

Produce An Awesome A-G-E-N-D-A

Just like a great Hollywood blockbuster movie your
agenda should have a great beginning, middle and end. One
way to do this is use the word 'A-G-E-N-D-A' itself to make
your next meeting agenda awesome.

A-G-E-N-D-A Outline

A - Attention Grabber
G - Great Goals
E - Excitement
N - Navigation Tools
D - Decide Now
A - Accountability Check-In

A - Attention Grabber

Every agenda should begin with an item that grabs everybody's attention. To get you started, here are a few
suggestions for how you can write your first
attention-grabbing agenda item:

- Make a short, honest statement about the company's
  current financial position and then talk about the fact
  that what you do in today's meeting can make it better
- Slam your fist on the desk and tell everyone to 'Wake
  up!'

- Have everybody stand up for the first few minutes of the meeting instead of remaining seated, and make sure you explain why you want to do this. For example you could say, "Our last meeting was really dull and we need to shake things up"

G - Great Goals

Every agenda that you produce should have great goals that move your organization strategy forward. Each goal that you put on the agenda should include the following components:

- The goal should have a great title that inspires people. For example, instead of writing 'Marketing Direct Mail Campaign Review' on the agenda, you could write 'Check Out The Highlights From The Most Effective Go-To-Market-Strategy We've Ever Had!' This approach is a simple way to sell your goals more effectively to your meeting team
- Each goal should be motivated by your strategic plan
- Every goal should be achievable within a reasonable number of meetings. For example, if you state that you want to find new customers in the first weekly meeting of the month, then by the last meeting of the month you should have some positive results

E - Excitement

Every agenda you build should be as exciting as your favourite Hollywood blockbuster movie. Here are a few suggestions that will help you achieve this:

- **Include inspirational quotes** that are connected to

the goals you are trying to achieve during your meeting. And if you do include a quote on the agenda I would also suggest that the facilitator practice saying it out loud before your meeting. This will allow him or her to say it with meaning

- **Include new project announcements** that are directly related to the outcomes of this meeting
- **List individual achievements** on the agenda, and set aside the proper amount of time to celebrate them during your meeting. You should also make a note in the agenda about how each individual achievement helped you move your organization strategy forward
- **Include positive stories** - For example, if your meeting team supports a charity, you could provide an update on how the charity is benefitting from your team efforts. Another way to celebrate a positive story during a meeting is to set aside time in the agenda to allow one of your team members to share a great story about someone else on the team. Then, as you accumulate more and more positive stories during your regular meetings, you will want to record them and revisit them at the end of the year
- **Include a note to serve refreshments during the meeting**, because nothing gets meeting teams more fired up than a free lunch!
- **Announce bonuses** that are tied directly to what you are achieving in your meetings

N - Navigation Tools

Every agenda should have a 'facilitator toolbox.' When I say toolbox I mean that you should include a checklist of relevant techniques that the meeting leader can use to optimize the discussion. Here are a few items that you can put in your 'facilitator toolbox' right now:

- **Zoom In/Zoom Out** - During a meeting a strong facilitator should be able to 'zoom in' to specific details. A strong facilitator should also be able to 'zoom out' and link those specific details to your organization strategy
- **Parking Lot** - During a meeting there are always useful ideas that come up that are unrelated to the goal of the meeting. So when this happens the meeting facilitator should be able to quickly acknowledge the idea and then 'parking lot' the idea for later, which means that it will be recorded during the meeting and reviewed at a later time

D - Decide Now

At the end of each agenda item you should include a reminder about whether or not you have to make a decision about what has been discussed. The reminder could be as simple as placing the word 'decision' into the agenda with a question mark, like this: 'Decision?' This is a great way to make sure that your discussions have meaning, rather than just being talk for talk's sake without seeing any results. It will also send a signal to your meeting team that they better be ready to make choices during the meeting.

A - Accountability Check-In

At the end of each meeting that I facilitate, I look each individual directly in the eyes and say, "Given what we have discussed today, what are you going to do about it when you leave this room?" This is a powerful accountability technique because everybody has to say out loud what they will do, and they have to say it in front of their peers. Once they do this, you now have a statement that you can track. Then you can follow up at the next meeting and ask them, "Did you do what you said you were going to do since our last meeting? And what happened?"

And if you think about it, it is rare that people make public declarations that they are accountable for. I have been to weddings and funerals where people speak from the heart and mean every word that they say. But so often in meetings we let each other off the hook. As a result there is no accountability, and if you don't have accountability you're going to keep having bad meetings.

A-G-E-N-D-A Example

With these A-G-E-N-D-A tips in mind, here is an example of how to put together an inspired agenda for a non-profit monthly board meeting.

1. **Attention Grabber** - Make the first agenda item an activity. For example, you could have individuals stand up and tell everyone something about themselves that nobody else could possibly know. This is a great way to get people engaged and build team trust
2. **Great Goals** - Write two key goals on the agenda and make sure you achieve them. For example:
    o **Goal #1**: 'Discuss how to raise $100,000 for programming needs and then assign people to follow up'
    o **Goal #2**: 'Determine whether or not we should actually ask for a vote to approve the minutes from the last meeting. Does anybody read

them? How will the minutes from our last meeting help us achieve our strategic objectives? If we actually require minutes from the last meeting, how can we make them more useful?

3. **Excitement** - Pump everyone up by including an inspirational quote on the agenda that will get the team excited about achieving Goal #1. For example, in relation to raising money for non-profits you could use this quote by Lauren Semple from Aching Arms, "Life is not scripted. Conversations with our donors should not be either."[41]

4. **Navigation Tools** - To assist the meeting facilitator you could make a note on the agenda about the Zoom In/Zoom out technique. Then the facilitator could actually use this technique to tie Goal #1 to your strategic plan. For example, when you 'zoom in' you might say "How can we acquire 50 donors in the first 90 days of the year?" Then when you 'zoom out' you might say, "Our fundraising goal for the year is $1 million, and we believe that acquiring 50 new donors in the first quarter will help us bring in $200,000, which will set the stage for raising the rest of the funds by the end of the year"

5. **Decide Now** - Before the meeting you could make a note on the agenda that ensures that you will ask everyone to make a decision after you talk about how to achieve Goal #1. For example, after you talked about the pros and cons of contacting 50 donors in the next 90 days you can decide if this should be done or not

6. **Accountability Check-In** - Before each person leaves the room they should declare what they are going to do between now and the next meeting that

will help your team acquire 50 donors in the next 90 days. Then, at the next meeting, you should ask them what actions they took to achieve this goal, as well as the results of their actions

A-G-E-N-D-A Example Follow Up

Imagine that preparing your next meeting agenda is like writing the script for a sequel to your favourite Hollywood blockbuster movie. If you do a great job, then your team will be even more enthusiastic about attending your next meeting. If you write a bad agenda then you can expect ticket sales to your next meeting to go down.

A-G-E-N-D-A Summary

A - Attention Grabber
G - Great Goals
E - Excitement
N - Navigation Tools
D - Decide Now
A - Accountability Check-In

Who Needs Awesome Agendas?

Awesome agendas can be used to make all kinds of meetings more profitable including:

- Board meetings
- Executive meetings
- Safety meetings
- Sales meetings
- Parent-Teacher meetings
- Weekly staff meetings

- Volunteer meetings
- Community meetings

If you don't have a plan, what sort of results can you expect from your next meeting?

How An Awesome Agenda Can Stop The 'Hidden Agenda'

Many meetings have a 'hidden agenda.' For example, someone may be intentionally trying to slow the meeting down. Or someone else may be holding back critical information that should be shared. One of the best ways to stop 'hidden agendas' is to list them on the actual agenda that you write. Then, when the meeting facilitator distributes the agenda before the meeting, everyone who is involved will see the 'hidden agenda' behaviours typed up on the actual agenda. Then, when the meeting starts you can read out the hidden agenda items, which will lead to a discussion with your team about how to stop any counter-productive behaviour.

In addition, here are a few more ways to stop the 'hidden agenda':

- Remove destructive people from the meeting
- Let people know that if they get past their 'hidden agenda' then your meetings will become more productive
- Create an incentive that will motivate the team to stop the 'hidden agenda' as in:
    - You'll be fired if you keep subverting our meeting efforts
    - We'll get a team cash bonus if we all stop

trying to sabotage each other

Hidden agendas are fun to watch in a Hollywood movie but they are a productivity killer in business meetings.

Agenda Editor

Every great Hollywood writer has a great editor. It should be no different when you're creating a meeting agenda. But one of the big mistakes that many meeting leaders make is that they create the agenda by themselves without asking for help. It is worthwhile to have others look at the meeting agenda before you send it out because:

- They will help you to think of things that you didn't
- They will help you to overcome your own bias, especially if you are tracking 'hidden agenda' items
- They will help you cut the agenda down to its essentials
- They will make sure that there are no spelling mistakes. Because we all know that simple spelling errors on team documents can erode overall confidence. Speling misstakes also become a distraction durring a meeeting because peopele will spend valuablle time talking about wronng words on the agenda instead of what yoo want to foccuss on (in the same way that trying to read this last sentence would drive most people crazy!)

Marketing The Agenda

Hollywood blockbuster movies would not succeed without a well-executed marketing campaign that exposes potential viewers to the movie in all kinds of ways, including movie trailers, entertainment shows, at fast food restaurants, in the supermarket, on the radio and other places where we are exposed to media. So if you want your next meeting to be as successful as a Hollywood blockbuster movie then you need to pre-sell the agenda to your meeting team. Here are a few promotional techniques to get you started:

- **Produce A Meeting Agenda Trailer** - Put together a short video that highlights what you are going to be talking about at the next meeting and send it out to your staff two days in advance
- **Cold Calling** - Call each person individually and deliver a simple, inspired message to get them excited about the agenda and the meeting
- **Mail The Agenda** - Send each person a copy of the blockbuster agenda in the mail. This will really get everyone's attention because who gets an inspirational letter in the mail these days?
- **Tantalizing Texts** - Send each person a brief text that will get him or her talking about your next meeting
- **Hallway Chats** - Plan a series of casual hallway chats with key influencers from around your office who you know will spread the word about the exciting things that will be happening in your next meeting. This is just like sending an advance screening copy of the movie to influential movie reviewers
- **Send A Survey** - You could do an online survey to ask your meeting team for their suggestions. For example, if you were planning to provide free pizza for a lunch meeting, you could send out a survey to ask the staff which kinds of pizza they would prefer
- **Get Reviews** - You could ask your team to review and rate your meetings, and if you get a five-star

review then you know you've created a blockbuster agenda.

- **Have A Contest** - For example, if someone is able to complete all of their tasks from the last meeting before the next meeting then they could win an iPad!

Step 6: Conclusion

What if every one of your meetings felt like your favourite Hollywood blockbuster movie? Like *Star Wars, Iron Man, The Wizard of Oz* or *Titanic?* Would it be worth preparing and promoting a blockbuster meeting agenda to make this happen? What if you could also use your meeting agenda to get rid of the 'hidden agenda?' Don't wait! Take action and create a blockbuster agenda that will excite your team and turn your meetings into a competitive advantage that will allow you to dominate your industry!

Step 6: Build A Blockbuster A-G-E-N-D-A Checklist √

1. Make your meeting agenda more exciting than your favourite Hollywood blockbuster movie
2. Write an awesome agenda 'story' that will grab your meeting team's attention and compel them to achieve their goals
3. Set aside the proper amount of time to prepare a blockbuster agenda and make sure to have it double-checked by a trusted team member
4. Build an exciting agenda marketing campaign, including great techniques such as doing a movie style 'agenda trailer' or asking your meeting team to review your meetings based on a 5-star system
5. Include useful navigation tools and techniques to help the meeting facilitator

6. Write the word 'Decision?' as often as possible on the agenda so that you will be reminded to take action
7. Use the Accountability Check-In to make sure that everyone states what they will do between now and the next meeting
8. Create an awesome agenda so you can stop the 'hidden agenda'
9. Figure out how you want to celebrate when your blockbuster agendas begin to consistently make your meetings more productive
10. Demonstrate how your blockbuster agendas are helping to improve your company's overall profitability

Tip: Check out Step 8 in this guide to find more awesome resources that will help you and your team 'Build A Blockbuster A-G-E-N-D-A'

Up Next

In "Step 7: Meet In The Right Space," you'll find out why holding meetings in the right place can make your organization more productive and profitable.

10

Step 7: Meet In The Right Space

Where You Meet Matters

Where do you hold your meetings? Is it an attractive space that leads to creative conversations and massive profits? Or does it have sticky seats, a dirty white board and old coffee stains on the table? Where you meet is as important as what you're meeting about. So if you want to inspire your team and make your meetings more profitable, then you should create an awesome meeting space. To get this process started, here are a few questions to consider:

Practical Questions About The Meeting Room

- Do we need to book the room?
- Is the room too hot? Too cold?
- Is the room clean?
- Does the room have a projector, screen, sound system, and connections for computers?
- What is the phone number for the audio/visual technician?
- Do we need a conference speakerphone?
- Do we need flip charts, markers, pens, pads, and sticky notes?
- Are the chairs in working order?
- Does the table move?

- Where are the electrical outlets?
- Do we need wireless Internet access?
- Do we need to order refreshments?
- Does anybody have special dietary considerations? Gluten-free? Vegetarian?

People Questions To Ask Before You Book The Meeting Room

- How many people are coming?
- Is there anything in the room that will distract us?
- Is everybody getting along?
- Should some people be seated apart from each other?
- Should some people be seated beside each other because they are doing excellent work together?
- If the manager sits at the front, what message does that send to the group?
- Does somebody know how to use the projector and sound system?
- Who is taking care of lunch?
- Who will take notes? Where will they sit?

"The biggest room in the world is the room for improvement."[42]

Author Unknown

Spatial Questions To Ask About The Meeting Room

- Can we all hear each other in this room?
- Can we see each other easily?
- What type of meeting is this? For example, is it a presentation style where someone stands at the front

and talks? Or is it a workshop where we'll need multiple tables and chairs so we can break out into smaller groups?

- How does our team like to meet? Standing? Sitting? Walking? In a boardroom? In a circle? In rows?

Inspiring Questions To Ask About The Meeting Room

- What do we want to see on the walls? Inspiring quotes? Funny sayings? Beautiful photos and artwork? Our team picture?
- Should we post our strategic Vision, Mission and Objectives?
- Does this space support the unique culture of our organization?

The Real Cost of Technical Difficulties

We've all been in that meeting where that guy says he has a great presentation...oh, and he just needs a minute to set up his PowerPoint slides...and then 15 minutes go by...a few people try to be helpful, calling technicians, pushing buttons...and as you add up the total cost of this meeting you realize you've just burned $1000 because that guy didn't bother to do a technical rehearsal before the meeting. Can you afford to waste meeting time due to technical difficulties? No. So I would suggest that you work with your team in advance to make sure that all technical issues are taken care of before each meeting.

How To Prepare For Meetings That Are Not In Rooms

Many people attend meetings that are not in rooms. For example, people might have meetings on a construction site or at a nursing station, and many people do walking meetings as a healthy alternative to sitting in a boardroom. Here are a few suggestions to help you get ready for meetings that are not in rooms:

Example 1 - On a Construction Site or out in the Wilderness

- Do you need a satellite phone to call into head office?
- Do you need remote Internet access?
- Will someone have to play a training video on a laptop that sits on the back of a truck? If so, what can you set up that will allow everyone to actually see it and hear it?
- Do you need electrical power?
- Are your laptop and cell phone batteries charged?
- Do you have the proper cords to charge all of your devices?
- Can you draw power from your truck?
- Do you need a gas-powered generator?

Example 2 - Open Area Meetings

Sometimes meetings are held in open areas like nursing stations in hospitals, or open-concept cubicle spaces in offices. To help you hold the most effective meetings possible in these types of spaces, here are a few suggestions:

- Do you have to keep your voice down so that the people around you who aren't in the meeting can't hear what you're saying?
- Are there too many distractions to have an effective meeting?
- Will you be dealing with sensitive information?

Example 3 - Walking Meetings

Walking meetings can produce highly effective results for a variety of reasons. To begin with, walking in the same direction literally supports the fact that your team is working together to arrive at a common solution. You are also getting your heart rate up, which allows you to think more clearly and creatively. And when it comes to solving problems, moving beats sitting. Here are some tips for conducting an effective walking meeting:

- Plan for the weather and dress accordingly
- Walk in a place that will inspire your conversation, like historical downtown, or on a great nature trail
- Choose a pace that suits everyone
- Leave your cell phone in the office so you don't have any distractions
- Tell everyone else at work about how productive walking meetings are, so that they will be inspired to try it
- Observe the impact of how walking in the same direction together helps you to connect more deeply with your team members

In-Town, Off-Site Meetings

Off-site meetings in your own city are worthwhile if they help you achieve your meeting goals. So, if you're thinking about getting out of the office to have a meeting in town, here is a list of pros and cons to consider:

Pros

- Off-site meetings remove day-to-day interruptions,

which allows for better focus and problem solving
- Off-site meetings provide a 'neutral' location so nobody will have an advantage
- Catering is provided so you don't have to worry about refreshments and meals, which will also create greater focus throughout your meeting
- If the food is good it can be a memorable highlight that motivates your team
- Off-site meetings can support local businesses that are related to your business, like hotels, historic sites, conference centres, sports centres, chambers of commerce and other venues
- You can take advantage of unique local opportunities, such as water parks, bowling alleys, gun ranges, paintball centers, archery clubs, go-kart tracks, day spas, and other fun or relaxing services
- This type of meeting is less expensive than taking the staff on an out-of-town trip

Cons

- Off-site meetings are more expensive than meeting at the office
- These types of meetings take your staff away from their regular duties, which they may like or resent, depending on their circumstances
- People often have to pay for transportation to get to the meeting
- The food could be bad, and that may be all that the staff ends up remembering about the off-site meeting

How To Overcome In-Town, Off-Site Meeting Objections

- Ask the staff to help you choose a great meeting place and an activity that everyone will enjoy
- Work with the off-site location staff to make sure that all the important details are taken care of
- Book an awesome guest speaker and let the staff know who it is in advance. For example, I was at an all-day conference and one of the last speakers was former Canadian Football League star Mike "Pinball" Clemons. He was awesome! Not only did he relate parts of his own life story to the theme of the event, he also passed around his CFL Championship ring for everyone to get a look at. His appearance was very memorable and served as a terrific energy boost at the end of a long meeting
- Use your blockbuster A-G-E-N-D-A (from Step 6) to promote why people should be excited about the up-coming off-site meeting

Destination Meetings

What would happen if you held your next meeting in Hawaii, Paris, Las Vegas or on a cruise? What sort of Meeting Return On Investment (MROI) would your company get? Would the people who went to your destination meeting become more motivated and productive? Which type of destination would help you get the best results? To help you decide, here is a list of pros and cons for destination meetings:

Pros

- Improve staff loyalty and retention because the staff feel they are being treated well
- Could be a once-in-a-lifetime trip for many of the

staff
- Could be a lot of fun and help you and your team get to know each other better, based on great activities, location and amenities
- The location could truly reflect your company culture and values. For example if you like to golf you could book an exclusive trip to the 'Old Course' in Scotland. If your team loves to shop, then you could book a destination meeting in New York

Cons

- Destination meetings are expensive
- You have to choose a superb destination with impeccable service, or else the focus will be about a bad trip experience instead of what you wanted to achieve in your meeting
- Destination meetings take people away from their families so they better be worth it
- It's hard to pick a destination that will please the whole team. For example, some people may think the destination is too extravagant, while others may think it's too cheap

Destination Meeting Tips

- Ask your travel agent to find group discounts
- Make special arrangements for individual staff issues, such as dietary considerations, and handicap accessibility for disabled persons

Conference Call And Webinar Meetings

Conference calls and webinars work well if everybody is

calling in from the right place. Because if someone is calling from his or her car, or a meeting participant is walking down the street and talking on the phone, or you can't hear what that person is saying because of a lousy microphone on their computer, then conference calls can be a nightmare. Here are a few questions that every team member can ask before attending his or her next conference call or webinar meeting:

- If I am calling from my home office, will my dog bark during the call?
- What is the quality of my microphone?
- Will everybody on the call be able to hear me?
- Can the moderator control the call, as in turn people on/off if necessary? (especially if somebody gets up to go to the bathroom and they don't turn off their microphone, which actually happened on a conference call with 300 people!)
- If most of the people on the call are meeting in a boardroom is there a speakerphone that works well? Does somebody know how to use it?
- Does everybody know the access code to get onto the call?
- Can the moderator manage all of the comments in the webinar chat room, or do they need an assistant to do this?
- Does everybody know when to speak up and when to listen?

I heard a funny story about a weekly corporate conference call that involved employees across North America. Every once in a while the people from the west coast office would say that they felt an earthquake tremor and that they had to leave the conference call early (even though there wasn't actually an earthquake). I guess that's one way to avoid a boring conference call meeting. And if you want to laugh out loud I recommend that you look up "David Grady: The Conference Call."[43]

Step 7: Conclusion

"Treat your home the way you treat your best friend"[44]

Rodika Tchi, Feng Shui Consultant

If you really want to inspire your staff and make your meetings count, you will invest in your meeting space and make it awesome. Not only will people feel great about the space they are meeting in, your Meeting Return On Investment (MROI) will improve.

Step 7: Meet In The Right Space Checklist √

1. Make a checklist of all the practical things to consider when you're setting up an exceptional meeting space
2. Be aware of who is attending the meeting and then be intentional about where they should sit, just like figuring out where people should be seated at a wedding
3. Go above and beyond to make the meeting space inspiring
4. Avoid technical difficulties by being prepared in advance
5. If you're not meeting in a room, then take the time to understand where you are meeting and get ready for it. And if you can, book a walking meeting and see what type of results you get

6.   Off-site-in-town meetings can be effective if they are well planned, so make sure to go over all the details well in advance

7.   Destination meetings can provide a great Meeting Return On Investment, but make sure that you assign a team to guarantee that all the details will be taken care of

8.   To make your next conference call or webinar seamless it is worthwhile to develop your own checklist and then make sure that everybody follows it

9.   If you have put the right amount of effort into setting up a great space, then make sure to celebrate the fact that it is now making your meetings more effective

10. Find a way to demonstrate that your new space is improving the overall profitability of your organization

Tip: Check out Step 8 in this guide to find more awesome resources that will help you and your team 'Meet In The Right Space'

Up Next

In "Step 8: Get Awesome Resources" you'll find awesome meeting tools and tips that will help you deepen your understanding of each step in this book.

11

Step 8: Get Awesome Meeting Resources

Why You Need Awesome Meeting Resources

No two meetings are the same. What worked for you last time may not work for you again. Because of this, you need a variety of tools to help you optimize every meeting you attend. So whether you're looking for ways to deal with difficult people, or inspiration to help you create your next business breakthrough, having the right meeting resources will help you do it more efficiently and profitably.

How To Use This Chapter

1. In this chapter, you'll find awesome resources to enhance your understanding of each step in this book. For example, if you want to find additional material to help you 'Get Real With Yourself,' then look up Step 1 in this chapter

2. If you're using the eBook or print version of "How To Create Awesome Meetings" and you want to look up one of the resources in this chapter, then all you have to do is enter the resource title text along with the quotation marks into your Internet browser. For example, if you want to find the article titled "How To

Pick A Good Fight," then type "How To Pick A Good Fight" into your Internet browser and you'll be able to find the article

3. If you're using the PDF version of "How To Create Awesome Meetings" and you want to look up one of the resources in this chapter then all you have to do is click on the title text with the quotation marks. For example, to find the article titled "How To Pick A Good Fight" just click on "How To Pick A Good Fight" and the article will pop up in your browser

4. And if you need any help finding any of these resources for your next meeting, please get in touch with me at gord@createawesomemeetings.com

Step 1: Get Real With Yourself - Resources

BOOKS

- "30 Self-Help Books That Helped Change My Life"[45]
  This well-researched article by Mandy Stadtmiller has a fantastic selection of self-help book titles to help you 'get real with yourself'

- "7 Habits Of Highly Successful People"[46]
  This superb self-actualization book by Stephen Covey has sold more than 25 million copies and is a personal favourite of mine

- "How To Win Friends & Influence People"[47]
  Since its release in 1936 this highly influential book by Dale Carnegie has sold more than 15 million copies

PODCASTS

- "15 Podcasts That Will Leave You Pondering Life's Big Questions"[48]
  This life-altering podcast list was put together by Alena Hall at HuffingtonPost.com

FUNNY VIDEOS

- "All The Best Bits // The Office US"[49]
  If you want to laugh out loud about meetings then check out these selections from the fantastic comedy series 'The Office'

Step 2: Get Real With Your Team - Resources

For 'Step 2A. How To Really Understand Each Person At The Team Meeting'

QUOTES

- "30 Quotes On Trust That Will Make You Think"[50]
  This article by Lolly Daskal on www.inc.com will help you think deeply about how to deepen your meeting team trust

For 'Step 2B. How To Really Understand Each Person At The Team Meeting'

VIDEO

- "The Power Of Introverts"[51]
  Find out why 'quiet' meeting team members are so important by watching this insightful Ted Talk by

Susan Cain on www.ted.com

For 'Step 2F. Learn How To Fight'

ARTICLES

- "How To Pick A Good Fight"[52]
  Find out why a peaceful workplace can be bad for business in this article by Saj-nicole Joni and Damon Beyer in Harvard Business Review on www.hbr.org

- "How Management Teams Can Have A Good Fight"[53]
  Find a variety of new tactics to help you and your meeting team deal with conflicts more effectively in this article by Kathleen M. Eisenhardt, Jean L. Kahwajy and L.J. Bourgeois III in Harvard Business Review on www.hbr.org

- "Why Young Firms Need Monday Morning Fights"[54]
  Find out why conflict is good in this article by James Allen in the Wall Street Journal on www.wsj.com

For 'Step 2G. How To Celebrate Real Team Meeting Results'

ARTICLES

- "Ten Fresh Ideas To Shake Up Workplace Celebrations"[55]
  Put some new life into your celebrations with this insightful article by Veronica Marsden in The Globe & Mail on www.globeandmail.com

- "10 Ideas For Celebrating Your Employees Personal

Milestones"[56]
Learn new ways to acknowledge outstanding individuals on your meeting team by reading this fresh article by the Young Entrepreneur Counsel on www.inc.com

- "Meeting Reboot: 20 Ideas To Freshen Up Company Gatherings"[57]
Get some new ideas to help you re-ignite your workplace celebrations in this article by Martha C. White on www.BizBash.com

BOOKS

- "Fierce Conversations"[58]
This authentic blockbuster book by Susan Scott has not only improved my facilitation work but it has positively influenced my life

- "Getting To Yes: Negotiating Agreement Without Giving In"[59]
This no-nonsense book written by Roger Fisher and William Ury will help you learn how to become a better negotiator

FUNNY TEAM MEETING VIDEOS

- "Bad Meetings by Join.Me"[60]
These videos on www.join.me will make you laugh until you cry, especially if your meetings are as bad as these!

Step 3: Know Your Total Meeting Cost $ - Resources

BOOK

- "Return on Investment in Meetings & Events"[61]
  Find out how to optimize the value of your meetings in this book by M. Theresa Breining and Jack J. Philips

Step 4: Get A Great Facilitator - Resources

BOOK

- "The Facilitator's Fieldbook"[62]
  This highly detailed book by Tom Justice and David W. Jamieson covers all aspects of facilitation and is a must-have resource for anyone who wants to run an effective meeting

Step 5: Link The Meeting To Your Strategy - Resources

LINKS

- "Create Your Business Plan"[63]
  This excellent tool will help any business owner or leader who wants to get started on their organization strategy. Offered by the US Small Business Administration

- "Using The Balanced Scorecard As A Strategic Management System"[64]
  The Balanced Scorecard approach by Robert S. Kaplan and David P. Norton is a must-read for any leaders who want to be certain that they have optimized their organization. Available in the Harvard Business Review on www.hbr.org

BOOKS

- "Business Model Generation: A Handbook for Visionaries, Game Changers, and Challengers"[65]
  If you want to understand and confront your business model so that you can make it the best it can be, then you have to read this insightful book by Alexander Osterwalder and Yves Pigneur

- "Successful Organizational Transformation: The Five Critical Elements"[66]
  If you need help guiding your organization through a major change, then it will be worthwhile to read this book by Marvin Washington, Stephen Hacker and Marla Hacker. Available on www.businessexpertpress.com

FUNNY VIDEO

- "The Expert (Short Comedy Sketch)"[67]
  This hilarious video by Lauris Beinert" will make you laugh until you scream out loud, because you will realize that you have been in this type of ridiculous meeting before!

Step 6: Build A Blockbuster A-G-E-N-D-A - Resources

LINKS

- "How To Design An Agenda For An Effective Meeting"[68]
  Find out how to use your agenda to quickly address meeting problems, in this excellent article by Roger Schwarz in Harvard Business Review on www.hbr.org

- "Creating Effective Agendas by The Ontario Ministry Of Agriculture and Rural Affairs"[69]
  This highly detailed meeting tool offered by The Ontario Ministry of Agriculture, Food and Rural Affairs will help you create an effective agenda

Step 7: Meet In The Right Space - Resources

DESTINATION MEETING LINKS

- "The World's Most Popular International Meeting Destinations"[70]
  Get great insights about where to book your next destination meeting in this article by Samantha Shankman on www.skift.com

OFF-SITE MEETING ARTICLES

- "6 Ways To Ruin A Company Off-Site Meeting"[71]
  Find out how to avoid disaster at your next off-site meeting in this article by Jeff Haden on www.inc.com

- "Secrets Of Planning A Terrific Off Site Meeting"[72]
  Get some down-to-earth off-site planning tips in this article by Anne Fisher on www.fortune.com

CONFERENCE CALLS

- "Career Boot Camp - 5 Tips To Lead Effective Conference Calls"[73]
  Learn the absolute essentials to make your next conference call successful in this article by Lisa Quast on www.forbes.com

FUNNY CONFERENCE CALL VIDEOS

- "David Grady: Conference Call"[74]
  If you're ready to laugh at all the mistakes that people make when they are on a conference call then you will love this video by David Grady on YouTube

- "A Conference Call In Real Life"[75]
  If you want to laugh out loud as you get ready for your next conference call then check out this funny video by Tripp and Taylor on YouTube

Step 8: Get Awesome Meeting Resources

LINK

- "Create Awesome Meetings"[76]
  Create Awesome Meetings offers tips, information and inspiration to make your next meeting more productive and profitable. Available on www.createawesomemeetings.com

Step 9: Follow Up F-A-S-T - Resources

DATA MANAGEMENT

- "SAP"[77]
  Find out how you can put your big data to work in real time at www.sap.com
- "DECK DecisionWare"[78]
  Save time and money with this flexible data solution by Spieker Point - www.spiekerpoint.com

Step 10: Take Action! Resources

ARTICLE

- "38 Of The Most Inspirational Leadership Quotes"[79]
  Get inspired by these great leadership insights in this article by Travis Bradberry on www.entrepreneur.com

- "8 Step Process for Leading Change"[80]
  Get the tools you need to lead a major transformational change with this 8 Step Process by John P. Kotter

VIDEO

- "Simon Synek: Why great leaders inspire action"[81]
  Find your 'why' by watching this unforgettable Ted Talk by Simon Synek on www.ted.com

Step 8: Conclusion

> "We become what we behold. We shape our tools and then our tools shape us."[82]
>
> *Marshal McLuhan*
> *Philosopher*

If you want great meetings, you need great tools. So don't wait! Start your research, talk to your colleagues and do everything you can to get the right resources to make your next meeting more productive and profitable.

And because this is the first edition of "How To Create Awesome Meetings" I would appreciate your feedback. Please let me know which resources worked best for you, and if you have any suggestions about more helpful meeting

resources, then please get in touch with me at
gord@createawesomemeetings.com.

Step 8: Get Awesome Resources Checklist √

1. Set aside some time to learn how to do proper meet-
    ing resource research. One of the best ways to get
    started on this is to consult with your local librarian
2. Share your meeting resources with your colleagues
    and friends, and ask them for their best suggestions
    in return
3. Check out the resource page on
    www.createawesomemeetings.com
4. Connect with your industry association to learn about
    how they're helping their members to have more ef-
    fective meetings
5. Ask your meeting mentor for great meeting resource
    suggestions
6. Get inspiration from a variety of sources beyond the
    Internet, including magazines, audio recordings,
    newspapers and libraries
7. Invest the time to find and read awesome books that
    will help you transform your meetings for the better
8. Choose funny and inspiring resources that will moti-
    vate your meeting team
9. Celebrate the fact that you have gone above and be-
    yond to bring in new knowledge that inspires your
    team to have awesome meetings
10. Make a list of all of the resources you have gathered,
    and then figure out how many ideas from these re-
    sources have actually been put to use in your
    meetings, and then assess how much more profitable
    your meetings have become because you were so
    proactive

Up Next

In "Step 9: Follow Up F-A-S-T" you'll learn the most profitable ways to take action after your next meeting.

12

Step 9: Follow Up F-A-S-T

"Don't put off until tomorrow what you can do today."[83]

Benjamin Franklin
A Founding Father of the United States

Why Follow Up After A Meeting

Do you follow-up after a meeting? If so, congratulations. And if not, here are a few reasons why you should:

- You'll make more money
- Your staff, customers, suppliers, mom, dad and anybody else who was in the meeting will be happier
- When you follow up after a meeting you get faster feedback, which can help you slow down if things are going wrong, or help you to capitalize quickly on things that are going right
- You'll deepen your trust level with everyone who was in the meeting, which will lead to higher productivity
- You'll improve speed-to-market for your products and services

Follow Up F-A-S-T

Congratulations! You've used the first 8 Steps in this

guide to create awesome meetings and now it's time to follow up and get rewarded for all of your efforts. To do this, I suggest you use the word F-A-S-T to remind you about the most important things you need to do right after a meeting.

F-A-S-T

F - Feedback Loop
A - Astonish Each Other
S - Standardize The Follow Up Process
T - Track Progress

F - Feedback Loop

Creating a rapid communication loop between the leader and his or her team is one of the best ways to follow up after a meeting. The faster that information about the meeting is passed between you and your team, the sooner you can take action. To create an effective feedback loop you should clearly understand your team's communication preferences. Instead of assuming that a mass email will get the message across you can ask your meeting team exactly how they want to exchange information, which may include:

- Individual emails
- Phone calls
- Informal hallway chats
- Office visits
- Handwritten notes
- Texting
- Social Media, including Twitter, Facebook, and LinkedIn

Feedback Loop Surveys

You can also get feedback by surveying your team in a variety of ways, including:

- Sending an online survey
- You can also hand out a photocopied set of questions at the end of the meeting and get handwritten responses
- Or you could post a 'hallway' survey. This is when you put a question up in a common area that people pass by frequently. Then people can put up sticky notes in response to the question. They can do it anonymously or openly, and within a week you can gather a lot of useful feedback

Meeting survey questions may include:

1. What worked or didn't work during the meeting?
2. How will that meeting help the company earn more money?
3. What was your opinion about the meeting space?

Make The Most Of Your Minutes

How important are meeting minutes? Have you ever been in a board meeting where this exchange happens?

Board Chairman: "Would anybody like to make a motion to approve the minutes from the last meeting?"
Director: "I will."
Board Chairman: "Will somebody second that motion?"
Director #2: "I will."

Board Chairman: "All in favour?" (and everybody on the board raises their hands). "Opposed?" (and nobody on the board raises their hands). "Motion approved."

Are you one of those people who raised your hand, but you didn't even bother reading the minutes from the last meeting? Do you send notes out after your last weekly staff meeting or your latest monthly executive meeting? Did anybody actually read them? And to the diligent minority that does read old meeting notes, my sincerest apologies, but for the rest of us PLEASE STOP THE MEETING MINUTE MADNESS!

If you are developing a useful Feedback Loop then you have to find the right balance for information tracking after meetings, because most of us don't make the time to read meeting minutes, but we would like to know the most important information from the last meeting. Here are a few suggestions about how to do this:

- Ask individuals on your team about the kind of format in which they would like to receive information from the last meeting. For example, they might say that they want the top three bullet points sent to them via group text directly to their phones. If you do this, then you'll know that the key information will get read and remain top-of-mind until the next meeting
- Don't assume that because you cc'd everybody in an email that they will actually read it
- Make the information from the last meeting valuable. For example, if you can connect what happened in the last meeting to your profits then people will pay more attention

A - Astonish Each Other

What would happen to your profits if you could astonish each other after every meeting? For example, what if someone stated what they would achieve at the end of your last meeting, and then they got it done a week early? This is a classic way to 'under-promise and over-deliver' that will inspire your whole meeting team. And what if they went a step further and showed everyone how their achievement was connected to your company's most important strategic objectives? Not only would the team be amazed by that person's individual achievement, but they would also gain a better understanding of how it connects to your company's 'big picture.' This is just one example of how to astonish each other, and here are a few more ways to amaze your team after a meeting:

- Send a handwritten thank-you note to a teammate who went above and beyond during a meeting
- During a hallway chat, publicly praise your colleague for what he or she accomplished during the last meeting so that everyone around you can hear the nice things you're saying about him or her
- Post your MROI – Meeting Return On Investment. For example, if the results of your last meeting helped your organization earn $100,000 then broadcast the results to the whole company
- Another way to get people excited about your meetings would be to calculate how much profit per minute you earned from your last meeting. For example, let's say your meeting cost was $1,000 for one hour. Then imagine that the profits generated by that meeting were $61,000. Now you could subtract the meeting cost from the profits like this;

$61,000 - $1,000 = $60,000. Then you could divide the leftover amount by sixty minutes like this; $60,000/60 minutes = $1,000 dollars of profit-per-minute. Imagine how your team would feel if they knew that their meetings were generating $1,000 dollars of profit-per-minute during a meeting?

S - Standardize The Follow-Up Process

McDonald's. Dunkin' Donuts. Hilton Hotels. These franchises are successful because they have standardized their systems. When you standardize your meeting follow-up process it will drive profitability in a similar way. Here are a few suggestions to begin the standardization process:

- Determine the best way to send mass communications that you know everyone will use consistently
- List positive wins in every communication you send out after a meeting
- Link each post-meeting communication to a targeted aspect of your strategic plan
- Set up a delivery schedule for your follow-ups. For example, within 24 hours we will give each other verbal feedback about the meeting. Then, within 3 days we will send out the key points via email, and so on
- Make sure that all issues from the last meeting are being addressed
- Create real consequences for people who don't follow-up

Also, you should be aware of over-standardization because it can be too time-consuming and not provide enough value. But if you realize that a higher level of follow-up after meetings will build profitability then it will be worth the effort.

T - Track Progress

Tracking results is one of the best ways to standardize your meeting follow-up process. This means managing both the hard and the soft data that you gather during meetings. So how are you managing your meeting data right now?

- In a spreadsheet?
- In a CRM (customer Relationship Management System)?
- Via some large Enterprise Resource Planning system?
- Where is your meeting data stored?
- Is someone assigned to track the meeting data?

Fluid vs. Static Data

Fluid data is updated in real time and can be accessed easily. Static data is sitting in paper files or on spreadsheets in someone's computer that nobody else has access to. So what type of data do you need to improve the profitability of your meetings? If you come up with a great idea during a meeting, where will you put that idea? How will it be tracked? Who will track it? How will it be activated?

Key Meeting Data Metrics

You should be able to link everything that happens during a meeting to a strategic objective. To make the most of a strategic objective you need to have fluid data that you can track, including:

- Time spent on a project

- Project status
- People assigned to the project
- Profit/loss
- Projected benefits

Strategic Objective Fluid Data Example

For example, let's say that you committed to building a new widget during a meeting. And you know that building this new widget supports a major strategic objective for your company, which is to 'bring new products to market.' A month later you could measure how what you discussed in the initial meeting is moving your strategic objective forward:

Project: Build a new widget

Strategic Objective: Bring new products to market

Results since our last meeting;

- **Time spent so far** - 30 days
- **Project status** – The completed prototype is ready for testing
- **People assigned** - Research and Development Team, Sales Vice President, Marketing Vice President, Chief Innovation Officer
- **Profit/Loss** - $250,000 sunk costs on Research and Development and Marketing so far
- **Projected benefits** - $10,000,000 gross sales in the first two years based on initial sales and marketing plan

Then, if you have an effective system to get real-time,

ongoing feedback about this type of data, you will have a better chance of making your new widget project successful.

One example of an easy-to-use data management system is called DECK DecisionWare[84] created by Spieker Point in Edmonton, Canada. This type of data management system provides easy-to-use dashboards that help you look at your data in a customized fashion. It's like driving your car. If you want to know how fast you're going or how much gas you have left, then you simply look at the dashboard to find out. This type of data management system can produce real time feedback about how your meetings are connecting to your strategic objectives, which will help you improve your profitability in a variety of ways, including:

- Capturing innovative ideas that came up during the meeting in relation to how they might generate a new revenue stream
- Capturing employee achievement moments that happen during meetings that you can then put to use when you decide about bonuses
- Determining any project's status in relation to what was talked about during your meetings

Data Traps And Solutions

Data entry is only as good as the users and the system you have in place. So don't rely on the meeting leader to also gather the data, because he or she is too busy to do this task well. Instead, assign someone who likes to gather and process data. Then you can encourage that person to boil your best meeting moments into customized strategic information that everyone can use to drive profitability.

F-A-S-T Example - After The Weekly Staff Meeting

With these F-A-S-T tips in mind here is an example of how to follow up after a weekly staff meeting.

1. **Feedback Loop** – Within 24 hours after the meeting the leader could make a brief contact with each key person. He or she could do this in a customized way based on how each person likes to communicate. For example, if one person likes to chat on the phone then the leader could call him or her, and if another person likes to text then the leader could send that person a text. The meeting leader could then summarize the most important feedback and add in his or her comments. After that, he or she could send a concise email to the meeting team that demonstrates the results of the Feedback Loop

2. **Astonish Each Other** - In an email sent out after the meeting the leader could announce that if the results of that meeting produce the right amount of profit, that everyone on the team will receive a $1,000 bonus

3. **Standardize The Follow-Up Process** - The meeting leader could consistently follow up like this after every profit-producing meeting

4. **Track Progress** - Three months later, the leader could use the results of that data to pinpoint the exact moment during that meeting when the profitable

5. project innovation occurred. The leader could then express how important that meeting was as he or she hands the $1,000 bonus checks to each individual on the meeting team.

F-A-S-T Summary

Here is a quick summary of how you can use the word F-A-S-T to help you effectively follow-up after a meeting.

F - Feedback Loop
A - Astonish Each Other
S - Standardize The Follow Up Process
T - Track Progress

Step 9: Conclusion

Invest In Follow-Up Or Don't Bother

Following up effectively after a meeting requires the right amount of time, resources and money. So if you're not going to budget for additional staff costs and a few hard costs, then following up properly will be very difficult. It all comes down to measuring the Opportunity Cost (see Step 3) of following up. Is it worth it? What would happen to your meetings if you did follow up effectively? What will happen if you don't follow up after your meetings?

Step 9: Follow Up F-A-S-T Checklist √

1. Don't put off until tomorrow what you can get done today
2. Figure out why it's worth following up by making a list of your 'top five reasons to follow up'
3. Ask your staff for feedback about your meetings and then take action on the most important things that you learn
4. Ask your staff about how they want to give and re- ceive feedback

5.   Astonish each other by following up quickly and efficiently
6.   Make a checklist so you can standardize your follow-up process
7.   Assign someone other than the meeting leader to gather data during meetings, and make sure they track the key points in a fluid data system
8.   Figure out the right level of money and resources you should invest to effectively follow-up after a meeting
9.   As your new meeting follow-up practices begin to produce productive results, make sure you take the time to celebrate this achievement
10. Demonstrate how following up after your meetings is improving profitability for your organization

Tip: Check out Step 8 in this guide to find more awesome resources that will help you and your team 'Follow Up F-A-S-T'

Up Next

In "Step 10: Take Action!" you and your team will be inspired to put everything you've learned into action so you can create awesome meetings!

13

Step 10: Take Action!

> "Do you want to know who you are? Don't ask. Act! Action will delineate and define you."[85]
>
> *Thomas Jefferson*
> *A Founding Father of the United States*

Raise Your Hand

Whenever I speak to an audience about 'How To Create Awesome Meetings,' I always ask them to "Please raise your hand if you love meetings." You know how many people raise their hands? Less than 5%...

Do you want to be one of the people who raises their hand because they love meetings?

Then take action today!

Find Your 'Why'

Before you can improve your meetings you need to figure out 'why' you should even try, because if your motivation isn't strong then nothing will happen. Here are a few prompts to help you discover 'why' you should improve your meetings:

- Your company is losing money, and one of the fastest ways to improve the situation is to start having more productive meetings
- You're losing your mind in useless meetings and if you don't do something about it you're going to quit or do something even worse
- You *hate* wasting time

Find Your Inspiration

Another great way to help you find your 'why' is to connect with people that inspire you. These may be people in your family, community, or they could be the larger-than-life icons that inspire us all. For example, I'm inspired by Terry Fox and here's why. In 1980, after Terry Fox lost a leg to cancer, he wanted to do something special to raise awareness and money for cancer research. So he started the Marathon of Hope during which he set out to run a marathon a day until he ran across Canada! What he accomplished was incredible. Not only did he run a marathon every day for 143 days, he also helped to raise millions of dollars, and inspire people around the world! Unfortunately, he only made it halfway across the country before cancer took his life. But his legacy of inspiration lives on and since he started his run more than $600 million has been raised in his name![86] Check out www.terryfox.org to learn more.

Here's a list of people to help you begin to discover who inspires you:

- Your Mom, Dad, Sister, Brother, Grandparents, Uncles, Aunts
- Steve Jobs
- Oprah Winfrey

- Martin Luther King
- Winston Churchill
- Your neighbour
- Gandhi
- Ernestine Shepherd
- Nelson Mandela

Another great place to find inspiration is from the people on your meeting team. For example, I used to work with a nice woman who did her job well. For many years I didn't know too much about her until I had a long talk with her at a company Christmas party. During that conversation I found out that she had used most of her modest salary to send money back home to her family in another country. That money was used to build a house for her parents and it was also used to help many of her family members to get an education! I was blown away because I never suspected that she was making this amazing sacrifice to help her family. She is a true inspiration to me to this day!

So, with that example in mind, I hope you take time to get to know the people in your meetings better because they could be your next great source of inspiration!

Inspire Your Meeting Team

Now that you've found your 'why' it's time to help your meeting team find a compelling reason to change your meetings for the better. You can do this by:

- Being positive during meetings
- Setting a great example that your meeting team can learn from

- Speaking honestly from your heart
- Preparing and delivering an inspirational speech that will motivate everyone to do their best. And if you're looking for a great example, then I suggest that you watch 'Steve Jobs Stanford Commencement Speech 2005.'[87]

Fail Faster

Try. Fail. Get feedback. Try again. And do this quickly. Because the faster you get rid of bad meeting practices, the sooner you'll find the right techniques to create awesome meetings for you and your team.

Create Small Victories

Before you can achieve big meeting improvements, you need to create a series of small victories. These small wins will give you and your team the traction you need to turn your meetings into a strategic, profit-driving machine for your company. For example, if a quiet person speaks up during a meeting, then take a moment to praise that individual. Or, if a chatty person manages to control themselves during a meeting and not waste time, you could take a moment to tell that person that he or she did well. Then, as your meetings become significantly more profitable you'll be able to look back at the small wins that added up to help you create awesome meetings.

10 Steps To Help You Take Action!

Another great way to create small victories that will help you improve your meetings is to carry out the 10 Steps in this guide. As a reminder, here are the key points from each step that will help you take action:

Step 1: Get Real With Yourself

- You can choose how you act during a meeting

Step 2: Get Real With Your Team

- You can build a deeper trust level with your meeting team

Step 3: Know Your Total Meeting Cost $

- Measure the total cost of every hour that you meet to remind you and your team that you can't waste a single minute during a meeting

Step 4: Get A Great Facilitator

- If you have a great meeting facilitator then do everything you can to keep him or her. If your meeting leader needs facilitation training then make the investment today and find that person the right course, the right mentor or hire a Professional Meeting Facilitator to help him or her learn. And if you have a bad meeting facilitator then you have to remove that person, or else you will continue to have unproductive meetings

Step 5: Link The Meeting To Your Strategy

- You should be able to stop at any moment during

your next meeting and easily demonstrate that what you're doing is moving your organization strategy forward

Step 6: Build A Blockbuster A-G-E-N-D-A

- Build awesome agendas that will make every one of your meetings more exciting than your favourite Hollywood blockbuster movie!

Step 7: Meet In The Right Space

- Improve your Meeting Return On Investment (MROI) by creating a space that will inspire everyone on your team

Step 8: Get Awesome Meeting Resources

- Fill your meeting toolbox with great techniques and information that will help you to achieve all of your meeting goals

Step 9: Follow-Up F-A-S-T

- Great companies do an excellent job of following up quickly with their customers. So you should treat everyone in your next meeting like they are your best customer, and then follow up with them quickly after the meeting so you can fix mistakes and take advantage of opportunities

Step 10: Take Action!

- Find your 'why'

- Inspire your team
- Learn the 10 Steps in this guide and start creating awesome meetings today!

Pay It Forward

After you have optimized your meetings then I recommend that you take what you've learned and 'pay it forward.' For example, you could offer your meeting expertise to your favourite non-profit group so it can run outstanding board meetings. You could also offer your expertise to other teams within your organization to help them improve their meeting profitability. With this 'pay it forward' approach not only will you be building meeting excellence capacity within your community, but you will also create a positive ripple effect that will be felt in meetings around the world.

Great Meetings Pay-Off

Great meetings will help you:

- Improve productivity
- Put more money in your pockets
- Improve staff spirit and retention
- Adjust your strategy quickly to help you get it right
- Have way more fun
- Build a better world

So what are you waiting for?

Take Action Now!

I work every day to make sure that more people have

better meetings because it's the best way that I know how to help people. I am 'changing the world, one meeting at time,' and I invite you help me achieve this goal by taking action and creating your own awesome meeting today!

Step 10: Take Action! Checklist √

1. Find your 'why' by creating a meeting motivation checklist
2. Get inspired by your favourite larger-than-life people from around the world
3. Get inspired by getting to really know the people on your meeting team
4. Be a great role model who truly demonstrates how to 'take action' and make your meetings awesome
5. Fail faster so you can find out what you need to know to improve your meetings as quickly as possible
6. Create a series of small wins that will eventually add up to a large victory
7. Learn the 10 Steps in this guide to create awesome meetings
8. 'Pay it forward' by sharing your meeting expertise with other organizations that need help
9. Plan to celebrate your awesome meeting achievements
10. Show how taking action is not only creating profitable results for your meetings, but also improving your organization's bottom line

Tip: Check out Step 8 in this guide to find more awesome resources that will help you and your team 'Take Action!'

About Gord Sheppard

Gord Sheppard is on a mission to create awesome meetings for you and your organization. With Gord, you can say goodbye to bad meetings and say hello to energized meetings with real conversations that build profitability!

During his 25 years of work experience, Gord has facilitated, run and participated in more than 2000 meetings. He is a Professional Meeting Facilitator, Consultant, Speaker and Author who combines a Master's Degree in Business Administration with a Bachelor's Degree in Drama, and Prosci Change Management Certification, to deliver a unique, people-centered approach that will help you make your next meeting more productive and profitable.

Gord is a proud husband, father, brother and dog-walker. He also loves hockey, playing guitar, mentoring and volunteering for worthy causes like www.100MenYEG.com.

You Can Hire Gord To:

- Facilitate your meetings
- Work as a Management Consultant to help you develop your organization strategy
- Do leadership development
- Coach your board of directors and your staff
- Speak at your event
- Do a customized meeting improvement workshop for your team

If you'd like to learn more about what Gord can do to help you make your meetings more productive and profitable, then get in touch with him at gord@createawesomemeetings.com, or learn more about his services at www.createawesomemeetings.com.

Testimonials

"Working with Gord has radically changed how I view my business and these changes are already leading to new growth for my company."

Alex Armstrong, Owner
Three Tall Women Design Inc.

"Over the years, I have been part of numerous planning sessions, but I have to say that Gord's ability to get straight to the point and see through all of the cloudiness is inspirational. He has an uncanny gift of being able to read individuals and situations, while bringing out their best in a very short amount of time. He helped us to produce great results that are truly actionable."

Cynthia Annett, Board Chair
Special Olympics Edmonton

"He is extremely detail orientated and pushes hard to get his projects accomplished efficiently and with great quality."

Lauren Aubry
Corporate Sales Associate, Promotivate

"Having worked with Gordon over a number of years on numerous television projects with the Motion Picture Arts Program at RDC, I can attest to the positive and well organized attributes of Gordon Sheppard. I am a big fan of this man and his talents. It's typical of my experience with Gord reading about how to organize productive meetings and celebrating positive outcomes. Gord is a man of action and encouragement and supported me when I'd go out on a limb. But he wasn't just another "rah-rah/group hug" guy. I trusted Gord to be insightful and to critique my efforts in a constructive manner and I must say he never let me down."

Larry Reese, Instructor
Red Deer College

"Having gathered a group of smart and powerful people to consult on a potential new project, I was nervous; these were not people with time to waste. I put my trust in Gord to create a meeting that would make good use of the time they were spending in the room that day, and he did not disappoint. Somehow, he simultaneously fostered a relaxed and casual atmosphere while keeping us on topic and on schedule. He ushered us through an extremely productive and rewarding conversation but never gave us any feeling of being controlled or overly formal. Not only did we accomplish our objectives, several of my attendees commented to me afterwards on the quality of the meeting and the facilitation. I'm grateful to have had Gord in my corner that day.

Nadine Riopel
Facilitator and Community Organizer

Thank You Pages

Because this book is 2000+ meetings in the making it would be impossible to thank everyone that contributed. But there are a select few that I must acknowledge because without their help this book would not have happened.

First of all I have to thank my family. To Tracy, my wife, thanks for your patience and encouragement. To Jack and Riley, thanks for listening to Daddy talk too much. To Freckles, thanks for taking me out for a walk when I needed to get away from the computer. To Gail, Joan, Christine and Matthew, thank you so much for your ongoing love and support. To Donna, Brad, Leslie, Ava and Max, thank you so much for your ongoing love and encouragement as well.

Thank you to my early-draft-reading friends and advisors including Alex Armstrong, Jeff Morton, Menasha Nikhanj, Mario Maier, Randy Nelson, Sheila Luther, Drew Carnwath, Don Cummings, Robert Casavant and Kathy Salmon.

Thanks to the Edmonton Public Library for the Writer in Residence Program through which I learned a lot from Elizabeth Withey, and also for providing a low cost way to print books on their Espresso Book Machine. And thanks to the Metro Writers in Residence Program through which I learned a lot from Gail Sidonie Sobat. And thanks also to the Canadian Authors Association, Alberta Branch, through which I gained a tremendous amount of insight, encouragement and assurance from Steven Ross Smith (Writer in Residence) and Suzanne Harris (Coach in Residence).

Thank you to the contractors who did an excellent job including Mack Mikclon and Elyne Quan, B. Rhiannon Adams and everyone on Fiverr.com.

I also have to send a huge shout out to the online mavericks that I have learned from and been inspired by; Pat Flynn, Chris Ducker, John Lee Dumas, David Siteman Garland, Amy Porterfield, Michael Hyatt, Jeff Walker, Joel Friedlander, Kimberley Grabas, Joanna Penn and Gary Vaynerchuk. I hope to meet you all at some point so I can thank you personally.

And finally to the Tim Hortons, McDonald's, Second Cup and Starbucks locations in my neighbourhood that have my butt print permanently embedded on their chairs. Thanks for not kicking me out as I worked on this book in your establishments for hours and hours and hours.

Special Acknowledgements

I cannot express enough thanks to the following people, and their representatives, for generously granting permission to quote their profound words in this book. They are all outstanding leaders and thinkers in their respective fields. And I would encourage you to check out their websites and learn more about them.

Brendon Burchard – *www.brendonburchard.com*

John Di Lemmi - *www.lifestylefreedomclub.com*

Victor Frankl - *www.viktorfrankl.org*

Rudy Giuliani – *www.bracewellgiuliani.com*

Tom Hopkins - *www.tomhopkins.com*

Marshall McLuhan - *www.marshallmcluhan.com*

John Naisbitt - *www.naisbitt.com*

Rodika Tchi – *www.rodikatchi.com*

Zig Ziglar – *www.zigziglar.com*

Appendix

Worksheet #1

Step 1 - Top 3 Self-Awareness Reminders

Record the top 3 things you need to keep in mind about yourself. Keep this list handy and refer to it before you go to your next meeting.

1.
2.
3.

Then follow-up after your meeting and track your progress for each self-awareness point.

1.
2.
3.

Worksheet #2

Step 2 - Meeting Team Traits Inventory (MTTI)

Meeting Description:

Meeting Goal:

Available Team Traits For This Meeting:

-
-

Team Traits That We Need To Get For This Meeting:

-
-

Observations:

-
-

Action Items:

-
-

Worksheet #3

Step 2F - Meeting Fight Guideline

We all agree that in order to fight effectively during our meetings we will:

-
-
-
-
-
-
-
-
-
-

Worksheet #4

Step 3 - Total Meeting Cost Per Hour

$ Wages per hour + $ Meeting Space Cost + $ Refreshments = $ Total Meeting Cost per hour

Meeting Type: '_____'

+ $ Wages for _____ people = $_____ per hour
+ $ Room Rental, Heat, Audio/Visual Equipment = $_____ per hour
+ $ Muffins/Bagels/Coffee = $_____ per hour
= $ A Total Meeting Cost of $_____ for one hour!

Index

Z

Endnotes

[1] Cynthia Annett's testimonial about Gord Sheppard.
http://createawesomemeetings.com/consulting/
[2] Baer, D. (2014). *37 Billion Is Lost Every Year On These 12 Meeting Mistakes*. Retrieved from http://www.businessinsider.com/37-billion-is-lost-every-year-on-these-meeting-mistakes-2014-4
[3] Frankl, V. E. (1985). *Man's Search For Meaning* – Washington Square Press, New York.
[4] Frankl, V. E. (1985). *Man's Search For Meaning* – Washington Square Press, New York.
[5] The Myers & Briggs Foundation – http://www.myersbriggs.org
[6] True Colors – https://truecolorsintl.com
[7] Celebrity Types – http://www.celebritytypes.com
[8] Burchard, B. (date unknown). As cited by McGregor, G. (2015). *The Value of a Marketing Mentor* – Retrieved from:
http://m.nzherald.co.nz/small-business-sme/news/article.cfm?c_id=85&objectid=11447182
[9] Million Women Mentors – www.millionwomenmentors.org
[10] The Esquire Mentoring Initiative – http://mentoring.esquire.com
[11] Wayne Gretzky official site – http://www.waynegretzky.com
[12] Walter Gretzky official site – http://www.waltergretzky.com
[13] Oprah's official website – http://www.oprah.com/pressroom/Oprah-Winfreys-Official-Biography
[14] The Oprah Show (no author cited; excerpt published on February 1, 1989) – The Teachers who Changed Oprah's Life – http://www.oprah.com/oprahshow/The-Teachers-Who-Changed-Oprahs-Life
[15] Newton, Isaac (date unknown). As cited by 'BBC Learning English'. Retrieved from - http://www.bbc.co.uk/worldservice/learningenglish/movingwords/shortlist/newton.shtml
[16] Ziglar, Zig. (date unknown). *The Little Book of Big Quotes*. P. 18. http://www.ziglar.com/sites/www.ziglar.com/files/bonuses/TheLittleBookofBigQuotes.pdf
[17] Ken Carter official website – http://coachcarter.com
[18] Coach Carter Plot Summary – http://www.imdb.com/title/tt0393162/plotsummary
[19] Author Unknown (date unknown). As cited by Picture Quotes http://www.picturequotes.com/trust-takes-years-to-build-seconds-to-break-and-forever-to-repair-quote-55
[20] Epictetus (date unknown) – As cited by Goodreads http://www.goodreads.com/quotes/738640-we-have-two-ears-and-one-mouth-so-that-we

[21] Euripides (date unknown). As cited by Quotationsbook.com -
https://books.google.ca/books?id=xZIKDlE74n4C&pg=PA6&lpg=PA6&dq=
%22The+good+and+the+wise+lead+quiet+lives.%22+Euripides&source
=bl&ots=s5aMGC48y4&sig=lgsVrQDeZ-
ShYGWh6TpQOTykc1A&hl=en&sa=X&ved=0CEUQ6AEwCGoVChMI__3VtM
X3yAIVq1s-
Ch0AbwZI#v=onepage&q=%22The%20good%20and%20the%20wise%2
0lead%20quiet%20lives.%22%20Euripides&f=false

[22] Robinson, K. (speaker). (2006, February). *Ted Talk – Do Schools Kill Creativity?*
https://www.ted.com/talks/ken_robinson_says_schools_kill_creativity?la
nguage=en

[23] Clark, F.A. (date unknown). As cited by Hay, D.C. (2003) – Requirements Analysis: From Business Views to Architecture. Pearson Education
Inc., publishing as Prentice Hall PTR. Upper Saddle River, New Jersey.
Retrieved from
https://books.google.ca/books?id=Qy6j2PemE8QC&pg=PR23

[24] Fight Club (1999) – http://www.imdb.com/title/tt0137523/

[25] Business Networking International – http://www.bni.com

[26] Author Unknown. (date unknown) – As cited on Special Dictionary
http://www.special-
diction-
ary.com/quotes/authors/a/author_unknown/a_job_worth_doing_is_worth
_doing_together.htm

[27] Drucker, P. F. (1957). *Landmarks of Tomorrow*. Harper & Row, New
York.

[28] Mankins, M.C (2014). Harvard Business Review article, *This Weekly Meeting Took Up To 300,000 Hours A Year*. Retrieved from
https://hbr.org/2014/04/how-a-weekly-meeting-took-up-300000-hours-
a-year/

[29] Baer, D. (2014). *37 Billion Is Lost Every Year On These 12 Meeting Mistakes*. Retrieved from http://www.businessinsider.com/37-billion-is-
lost-every-year-on-these-meeting-mistakes-2014-4

[30] Naisbitt, J (1982). *Megatrends*. Warner Books, New York.

[31] International Association of Facilitators – Retrieved from
https://www.iaf-world.org/site/home/about

[32] The Masterful Facilitation Institute – Retrieved from
http://masterfulfacilitation.com/subpage/about-
us/missionapproach#axzz3nTA90bLO

[33] Reference to SFU's facilitation course – Retrieved from
http://www.sfu.ca/continuing-studies/courses/dlog/effective-group-
facilitation.html -

[34] Hopkins, T. (date unknown). Retrieved from Tom Hopkins' official website home page - http://www.tomhopkins.com/free_resources.shtml

[35] Di Lemme, J (2015). Retrieved from official John Di Lemme blog –
http://johndilemmeblog.com/tag/success/page/3/

[36] Carroll, L. (1865); Tenniel, J; Irwin, M. (1992). Paraphrase of exchange between Cheshire Cat and Alice in CH 6 - *Alice in Wonderland.* Wordsworth Classics Edition, Ware, Hertfordshire, England.

[37] Giuliani, R. (2008). *Transcript: Former New York Mayor Rudy Giuliani* (September 3, 2008) – Retrieved from http://www.npr.org/templates/story/story.php?storyId=94254610

[38] de Saint- Exupéry, Antoine (date unknown). As cited by Goodreads – https://www.goodreads.com/author/quotes/1020792.Antoine_de_Saint_Exup_ry

[39] Dyck, B.; Neubert, M. (2009). *Management: Current Practices and New Directions* – Houghton Mifflin Harcourt Publishing Company, Boston, MA. Retrieved from http://books.google.ca/books?id=87NsCgAAQBAJ&pg=PA4&lpg=PA4

[40] Kennedy, M. (2014). *The Lion King Earns Record Box Office.* Retrieved from http://bigstory.ap.org/article/1050ff927d15435d8ab25e7f1b1b5ebe/apnewsbreak-lion-king-makes-history

[41] Semple, L. (date unknown). Retrieved from http://www.stelizabeths.org.uk/get-involved/fundraising/ and http://101fundraising.org/2014/02/25-awesome-fundraising-quotes/

[42] Anonymous (date unknown). As cited by izQuotes - http://izquotes.com/quote/354053

[43] Grady, D. (2010). The Conference Call. Retrieved from https://www.youtube.com/watch?v=zbJAJEtNUX0

[44] Tchi, R. (date unknown) – Retrieved from https://www.pinterest.com/pin/350577152221868850/

[45] Stadtmiller, M (2014). *30 Self-Help Books That Permanently Changed My Life.* Retrieved from http://time.com/3478972/self-help-books-permanently-changed-my-life/

[46] Covey, S. (1989) *The 7 Habits of Highly Effective People.* https://www.stephencovey.com/7habits/7habits.php

[47] Carnegie, D. (1936). *How To Win Friends and Influence People.* http://www.dalecarnegie.com/about-us/dale-carnegie-books/

[48] Hall, A. (2015). *15 Podcasts That Will Leave You Pondering Life's Big Questions. Retrieved from* http://www.huffingtonpost.com/2015/01/08/top-mindful-podcasts_n_6423426.html

[49] The Office U.S. official YouTube channel - Retrieved from https://www.youtube.com/playlist?list=PLdVY0007sCPX9B5mlEOs2TZpVzgPKVMN1

[50] Daskal, L. (2015). *Trust Me, These 30 Quotes About Trust Could Make a Huge Difference.* Retrieved from http://www.inc.com/lolly-daskal/trust-me-these-30-quotes-about-trust-could-make-a-huge-difference.html

[51] Cain, S. (2012) – Ted Talk - The Power of Introverts – Retrieved from http://www.ted.com/talks/susan_cain_the_power_of_introverts?language=en

[52] Joni, S.N.; Beyer, D. (2009). Harvard Business Review article, *How to Pick a Good Fight*. Retrieved from https://hbr.org/2009/12/how-to-pick-a-good-fight

[53] Eisenhardt, K. M.; Kahwajy, J.L.; Bourgeois (III), L.J. (1997). Harvard Business Review article, How Management Teams Can Have a Good Fight. Retrieved from https://hbr.org/1997/07/how-management-teams-can-have-a-good-fight

[54] Allen, J. (2015). Wall Street Journal article, *Why Young Firms Need Monday Morning Fights. Retrieved from* http://blogs.wsj.com/experts/2015/05/27/why-young-firms-need-monday-morning-fights/

[55] Marsden, V. (2014). The Globe and Mail article, *Ten Fresh Ideas To Shake up Workplace Celebrations*. Retrieved from http://www.theglobeandmail.com/report-on-business/small-business/sb-tools/top-tens/ten-fresh-ideas-to-shake-up-workplace-celebrations/article18908245/

[56] Author: Young Entrepreneur Council/various (2015). Inc.com article, *10 Ideas for Celebrating Your Employees' Personal Milestones*. Retrieved from http://www.inc.com/young-entrepreneur-council/10-ideas-for-celebrating-your-employees-personal-milestones.html

[57] White, M.C. (2014). BizBash article, *Meeting Reboot – 20 Ideas to Freshen Up Company Gatherings*. http://www.bizbash.com/meeting-reboot-20-ideas-to-freshen-up-company-gatherings/new-york/story/29634/

[58] Scott, S. (2002). *Fierce Conversations*. The Berkley Trade Group, New York. Scott, Susan http://www.fierceinc.com/resources/books

[59] Fisher, R.;Ury, W.L. (1981). *Getting To Yes*. Penguin Books, City of Westminster, England. http://www.williamury.com/books/getting-to-yes/

[60] Join.me - group (2011). *Bad Meetings* comedy video – Retrieved from https://www.youtube.com/watch?v=nl44c78T4HU&index=2&list=PL27tS4BYpJcHvZsscnLCTnIcjGlbbeGWt

[61] Breining, T; Philips, J. J.; Philips, P.P. (2012). *Return On Investment in Meetings and Events. Routledge, London.* http://www.amazon.ca/Return-Investment-Meetings-Theresa-Breining/dp/0750683384

[62] Justice, T; Jamieson, D.W. (2012). *The Facilitator's Fieldbook*. AMACOM, New York. http://www.amazon.ca/The-Facilitators-Fieldbook-Tom-Justice/dp/0814420087

[63] Link to help you create your business plan - https://www.sba.gov/writing-business-plan

[64] Kaplan, R.S.; Norton, D.P. (2007). Harvard Business Review article, *Using The Balanced Scorecard As A Strategic Management System*. Retrieved from https://hbr.org/2007/07/using-the-balanced-scorecard-as-a-strategic-management-system

[65] Osterwalder, A.; Pigneur, Y. (2010). *Business Model Generation: A Handbook for Visionaries, Game Changers, and Challengers*. Wiley, New York. http://www.businessmodelgeneration.com/book
[66] Washington, M; Hacker, S; Hacker, M (2011). *Successful Organizational Transformation: The Five Critical Elements*. Business Expert Press, United States. http://www.businessexpertpress.com/books/successful-organizational-transformation-five-critical-elements
[67] Beinerts, L. (2014). *The Expert* (Short Comedy Sketch). Retrieved from https://www.youtube.com/channel/UCc70aB6IfdZpR6mlTON1qjg?sub_confirmation=1
[68] Schwarz, R. (2015). Harvard Business Review article, *How To Design An Agenda For An Effective Meeting*. Retrieved from https://hbr.org/2015/03/how-to-design-an-agenda-for-an-effective-meeting
[69] *Creating Effective Agendas* by The Ontario Ministry Of Agriculture and Rural Affairs http://www.omafra.gov.on.ca/english/rural/facts/05-037.htm
[70] –Shankman, S , (2013). Skift.com article, *The World's Most Popular International Meeting Destinations*. Retrieved from http://skift.com/2013/05/16/the-worlds-most-popular-international-meeting-destinations/
[71] Haden, J. (2012). Inc.com article, *6 Ways To Ruin A Company Off-Site Meeting*. Retrieved from http://www.inc.com/jeff-haden/6-ways-to-ruin-a-company-offsite-meeting.html
[72] Fisher, A. (2011). Fortune.com article, *Secrets Of Planning A Terrific Off Site Meeting*. Retrieved from http://fortune.com/2011/12/21/secrets-of-planning-a-terrific-off-site-meeting/
[73] Quast, L. (2013). Forbes.com article, *Career Boot Camp: 5 Tips To Lead Effective Conference Calls*. Retrieved from http://www.forbes.com/sites/lisaquast/2013/03/18/career-boot-camp-5-Tips-to-lead-effective-conference-calls/
[74] Grady, D. (2010). The Conference Call. Retrieved from https://www.youtube.com/watch?v=zbJAJEtNUX0
[75] Crosby, T. (2014). Comedy video, *A Conference Call In Real Life*. https://www.youtube.com/watch?v=DYu_bGbZiiQ
[76] Website for Create Awesome Meetings - by Gord Sheppard - www.createawesomemeetings.com
[77] SAP SE - www.sap.com
[78] Deck DecisionWare by Spieker Point. www.spiekerpoint.com
[79] Bradberry, T. (2015). Entrepreneur.com article, *38 Inspirational Quotes*. Retrieved from http://www.entrepreneur.com/article/244674
[80] Link to 8 Step Process for Leading Change. Retrieved from http://www.kotterinternational.com/the-8-step-process-for-leading-change/
[81] Synek, S. (2009). Ted Talk - *Simon Synek: Why great leaders inspire action*. Retrieved from

http://www.ted.com/talks/simon_sinek_how_great_leaders_inspire_actio n?language=en

[82] McLuhan, M (1994). *Understanding Media: The Extensions of Man*. P. xxi. MIT Press, Cambridge, United States. Retrieved from http://www.uq.edu.au/ccsc/understanding-media-the-extensions-of-man

[83] Franklin, B. (date unknown). As cited by Schwartz, D.J. (1987). *The Magic of Thinking Big*. Simon & Schuster, Riverside, NJ. Retrieved from https://books.google.ca/books?id=VaPNBAAAQBAJ&pg=PT161

[84] Deck DecisionWare by Spieker Point – www.Spiekerpoint.com

[85] Jefferson, Thomas (date unknown). As cited by Goodreads https://www.goodreads.com/quotes/21623-do-you-want-to-know-who-you-are-don-t-ask

[86] All biographical information retrieved from Terry Fox's official website – http://www.terryfox.org/TerryFox/Facts.html

[87] Jobs, S. (2005). Stanford Report, *Transcript of Steve Jobs speech at Stanford University on June 12, 2015*. Retrieved from http://news.stanford.edu/news/2005/june15/jobs-061505.html